Real Happiness

Proven Paths for Contentment, Peace & Well-Being

by

JONAH PAQUETTE, Psy.D.

"Dr Jonah Paquette's book offers a fresh, insightful, and enjoyable read on the important topic of well-being. It is replete with fun-to-read stories about the issues that surround the complex subjects of social intelligence and happiness. This book eloquently and easily gets to the heart of a topic that philosophers have mused about for thousands of years. Dr. Paquette offers the reader thoughtful and valuable guidance for what we all hope to achieve in life."

-**John B. Arden, PhD** author of *Brain2Brain*, *The Brain Bible*, and *Rewire the Brain*.

"Beautifully written and scientifically rigorous! Jonah Paquette presents readers with the latest in the science of happiness, and does it in a way that is both accessible and practically useful."

-**Acacia C. Parks, PhD** Assistant Professor of Psychology, Hiram College, & Scientific Advisor to Happify.com

"I've probably read most books on the topic of happiness and found this to be a unique blend of scientific research, practical advice, and entertaining and relevant personal stories. Happiness seems like something that should be easy to achieve and yet remains elusive for most of us. Jonah Paquette is honest about the effort, intention, and discipline required if one truly wants to be happier and offers simple strategies and exercises rooted in scientific research to help you improve your emotional well-being and feel more content, optimistic, and yes, happier!"

-**Nataly Kogan**, co-founder and CEO, Happier Inc.

Copyright © 2015 by Jonah Paquette, Psy.D.

Published by
PESI Publishing & Media
PESI, Inc
3839 White Ave
Eau Claire, WI 54703

Cover Design: Amy Rubenzer
Layout Design: Bookmasters
Edited By: Marietta Whittlesey

Printed in the United States of America

ISBN: 978-1-55957-015-2

PESI
Publishing
& Media
www.pesipublishing.com

Table of Contents

Acknowledgements

No book is produced in a vacuum, and it goes without saying that the creation of this book would have been impossible without the help and support of countless colleagues, friends, and family members. Unfortunately, the list of people whom I am indebted to far exceeds the space allotted for this brief section. But despite these constraints, there are a handful of individuals I'd like to thank for their guidance and encouragement throughout the writing process.

To my incredible team at PESI Publishing: Linda Jackson, Hillary Jenness, and Marietta Whittlesey. Thank you for helping to turn my manuscript into a cohesive and coherent book, and for making a potentially daunting process feel enjoyable and smooth.

To my gifted and brilliant colleagues: Steve Priebe, Doris Gates, Stephanie Snyder, and Lisa Kuhlman. Thank you for your wisdom, kindness, and compassion.

To my patients, both past and present: Thank you for letting me share in your inner world, and thank you for allowing me to witness your strength, courage, and perseverance.

To my parents, Gregory and Kathy Paquette: Thank you for your love, generosity, and support over the years. And thank you for always believing in me.

To my brother, Gabriel Paquette: Thank you for being the best "big bro" I could ever ask for. And thank you for inspiring me with your intellect and work ethic.

And to my beautiful and talented wife, Kelly Paquette: Thank you for supporting me through the lengthy process of writing a book. And thank you for showing me what true courage looks like, and what true love feels like.

Author Bio

 Jonah Paquette, Psy.D., is a clinical psychologist, author, and speaker. He works for Kaiser Permanente in California, where he conducts individual and group psychotherapy, and also provides clinical supervision for trainees. A graduate of Columbia University, Dr. Paquette completed his doctoral training at the PGSP-Stanford Psy.D. Consortium in Palo Alto, California. He currently resides in Marin County with his wife. To learn more about Dr. Paquette, please visit his website at www.jonahpaquette.com.

Introduction

"Happiness depends upon ourselves."

—Aristotle

WHAT'S IN A SMILE?

On a warm spring day in 1958, the graduating class at Mills College stood before a photographer to pose for their annual yearbook photo. The women who constituted the senior class at this private women's college in California were in most ways no different from any other graduating class across the country. Some of them would perhaps go on to become schoolteachers, others would pursue careers in nursing, and still others would start their own businesses. Many would go on to get married, while others would not. And some would achieve their hopes and dreams, whereas others would go on to struggle with pain and heartbreak.

But while this graduating class shared many similarities with others across the country, there was one key difference: The women at Mills College were in fact enrolled in a long-term study of major life events, such as marriage, motherhood, and life satisfaction. And it was this small difference that enabled this particular graduating class to provide exciting and crucial clues about the nature of happiness, and its importance in our lives.

****

Think about the last time you've posed for a picture. Perhaps it was during a night out with friends, at a recent family gathering, or with a loved one. Do you remember how you smiled? As we all know, there are many ways to smile for the camera when the person taking our picture says, "cheese." There's that big, genuine and robust smile we flash when we feel joyful and happy. And then there's the strained, somewhat forced smile we might give when our mind is elsewhere, or if we are compelled to take a picture next to someone we don't particularly like.

As it turns out, scientists have distinguished between these types of smiles, and refer to them as "Duchenne" and "non-Duchenne" smiles, respectively. These terms refer to the French physician Guillaume Duchenne, who was the first to identify the difference between these two ways of smiling. A Duchenne smile involves both the muscle groups surrounding our mouths as well as those around our eyes, resulting in a full-faced and genuine expression of happiness (often complete with "crow's feet"). A non-Duchenne smile, on the other hand, involves only the muscles around our mouth and is not considered to reflect positive emotions to the same degree.

How we smile might not seem like such a big deal, but it turns out to have some pretty fascinating and crucial implications. Returning to our subjects at Mills College, we might imagine that some of them gave broad, full smiles for their yearbook photos while others did not. But does that really matter? And more importantly, would it actually tell us something about these women on a broader level, and provide clues about how they might fare in the years ahead?

It so happens that two researchers at UC Berkeley, Dacher Kelter and LeeAnne Harker, were interested in these very questions. I mentioned earlier that members of the graduating class at Mills College were already enrolled in a long-term study examining major events in their lives, from marital status to their employment. This meant that the researchers already possessed data regarding how these women had fared in the years that followed their graduation, in some cases decades later. Keltner and Harker were interested in whether or not the nature of a person's yearbook smile was in fact connected to her future success in areas such as marriage, relationship satisfaction, career achievement, and life satisfaction.

The team of researchers began their quest for answers by examining the yearbook photos of 114 members of the graduating class. They then rated these photos according to the level of "Duchenne-ness" evident in the women's smiles, on a one through 10 scale. After doing so, Harker and Keltner aimed to determine how, if at all, a person's level of happiness as evidenced by a yearbook photo, was in fact connected to the sorts of major life events outlined above. Their results were nothing short of remarkable.

The women whose smiles were rated highest in terms of their "Duchenne-ness" were more likely to be married, and their marriages were more likely to be described as satisfying. Furthermore, they scored higher in terms of their overall life satisfaction and ability to handle stress. Moreover, the researchers were able to control for physical attractiveness, meaning we know that this wasn't the factor underlying these positive life developments. As if these findings weren't impressive enough, it turns out that these differences remained true even after *decades* had passed. In short, a young woman expressing happiness in her early twenties, even for just that brief moment in time, would be far more likely to succeed in life and love decades later. And all of this from a yearbook photo!

You may be wondering whether there's something unique about college-aged individuals, or whether this finding would hold true if the subjects were male. As it happens, another team of researchers were interested in whether the results of the "yearbook study" outlined above could in fact be generalized to other walks of life. To do so, professors Ernest Abel and Michael Kruger of Wayne State University chose, of all things, baseball cards to examine the level of "Duchenne-ness" of ballplayers' smiles. This particular study caught my interest not only as a psychologist but also as a lifelong baseball fan, as it may for any of you out there who collected baseball cards when you were growing up.

Abel and Kruger examined photographs of major league baseball players from the 1952 season and, similarly to the study above, they sorted these players according to their smiles. However, rather than looking at variables like marital outcome and life satisfaction, they instead chose to see whether there might be a connection between the types of smiles exhibited by players in their photos and their longevity.

Remarkably, the researchers discovered a huge connection between a player's smile and his lifespan. Specifically, players who displayed no smile in their photo lived an average of 72 years, while players who showed a slight smile lived until the age of 75 on average. Most strikingly, those players who were deemed to be displaying Duchenne smiles lived on average until 80 years of age. When I was a child collecting baseball cards of my favorite players, I would study them intently looking for evidence and data about who the best players were. Little did I know at the time, I was also looking at clues about who might live the longest.

****

What do findings like the "yearbook study" and the "baseball card study" tell us? Above all, they underscore the importance of being happy. Although a smile in a photo represents only a thin slice of time in a person's life, it can nonetheless provide valuable clues about the relative cheerfulness and level of happiness of the person being photographed. We often think of happiness as being a worthy end goal in and of itself, but one of the most exciting findings in recent years has been the discovery of the connection between being happy and a number of other desirable results in our lives. As the studies above show, being happy can also mean living longer, strengthening our relationships, achieving our career goals, and having greater life satisfaction. And after all, who wouldn't want that?

We all want to be happy. If you were to ask the average person on the street what they want most, there'd be a high likelihood they'll respond with happiness as their answer. Ed Diener, a psychologist and one of the world's foremost experts on happiness, points out that throughout the world personal happiness ranks at or near the top of most people's list of what they want in life. Most of our major decisions, including marriage, having children, buying a bigger house, or changing jobs, are done with our happiness in mind. But what is happiness? Is it something we are born with or is it something we can create? And is it something that we can actually influence in a lasting and meaningful way?

These questions, and more, will be answered in the coming pages of this book. In the first section, we'll explore the nature of happiness, the benefits of being happy, and review some of the barriers that often stand in our way of happiness. We will also discuss what we can and can't accomplish when it comes to lastingly changing our happiness level, and review ways in which you can personalize the content of this book to fit your unique happiness goals.

In the second section of this book, we will introduce and review seven scientifically proven principles that have been shown to boost our happiness levels in lasting ways. This will include both a brief overview of the important research findings relevant to these principles, as well as a discussion of the benefits of practicing them. Most importantly, we will introduce practical and concrete techniques to help you implement these concepts into your life starting today.

Can you become lastingly happier, and achieve greater joy and purpose in your life? Absolutely. It will take effort and hard work, but with that commitment comes the promise of finding levels of well-being and happiness far beyond your experience to this point. From the bottom of my heart, thank you for joining me on this journey. I hope and expect that it will prove to be worthwhile.

The Pursuit of Happiness

"What is the meaning of life? To be happy and useful."

—His Holiness, the Dalai Lama

WHAT IS HAPPINESS?

What does the word "happiness" mean to you? What are the emotions, experiences, and images that it brings to mind? One of the challenges of helping people become happier is that the very notion of happiness is often difficult to define. Indeed, people throughout history have offered vastly different opinions about the nature of happiness and how to achieve it. Mahatma Gandhi believed that happiness occurs "when what you think, what you say, and what you do are in harmony." Conversely, the French philosopher and physician Albert Schweitzer memorably declared that happiness is "nothing more than good health and a bad memory." But what is happiness, really?

Many of us may feel we don't need a formal definition of happiness because it's so innate, and rooted in common sense. Yet for the purpose of this book, and to get on the same page, it's helpful to have at least a broadly shared concept of happiness and psychological well-being.

One of the world's foremost happiness researchers, psychologist Martin Seligman, has described happiness as comprising three distinct yet interconnected parts: positive emotions, engagement, and meaning. "Positive emotions" refers to pleasant feelings about our past, present, and future and is marked by good cheer and positive sentiments. "Engagement" refers to the idea of a state of flow, where we are so engrossed in what we are doing that time seems to stop. Consider a time, for example, when you were perhaps playing a sport, playing an instrument, or doing a task such that you were "one with it." Lastly, "meaning" in this context alludes to being involved in, or serving something, greater than yourself. This might include, for example, your church, a community organization, or a cause you believe in passionately.

Whereas the "Hollywood" depiction of happiness is marked by ebullience and extreme positive emotions, according to Seligman positive emotions are in fact the least important components of lasting happiness. To borrow a metaphor, they are merely the cherry on top of our happiness sundaes. Far more important in his view of helping us achieve the good life are the ideas of engagement and meaning. Another accomplished happiness researcher, Sonja Lyubomirsky, posits that happiness is the "experience of joy, contentment, or positive well-being, combined with a sense that one's life is good, meaningful, and worthwhile." Much like the definition provided by Seligman, her description underscores the multiple layers of true happiness. It captures the importance of both positive emotions and a deeper sense of meaning and purpose in our lives. Combining these definitions for the purpose of this book, we will consider happiness and well-being to consist of:

- A strong presence of positive and pleasant emotions, both in the present moment as well as towards the past and the future
- A feeling of connection to those around us, as well as to our activities, pursuits, and vocations
- An underlying feeling of satisfaction with our life
- A deep sense of meaning and purpose that anchors us even when our more fleeting positive emotions are not present

In the pages that follow, we will be using the terms *happiness* and *well-being* interchangeably, and we will be drawing on the definitions outlined above. The type of happiness you will build as a result of reading this book will consist of not only positive emotions and feeling good, but also a deeper sense of connectedness, meaning, and engagement in your life.

AN OLD AND NEW PURSUIT

The quest for happiness is not a new one, and has in fact been a concern of philosophers, thinkers, and theologians for centuries. Indeed, many of the questions we are addressing in this book have been asked for thousands of years all around the world. From Buddhist and Confucian scholars in the East, to Greek and Roman philosophers in the West, issues such as happiness and the "good life" have been at the forefront of human inquiry as far back as we can look. It is on the shoulders of these thinkers that many of the contemporary findings regarding happiness stand.

Within the field of psychology, much focus has traditionally been centered on the reduction of misery and managing psychological illness. This has yielded a great deal of progress in terms of managing the symptoms of mental illness, and in fact many disorders that were once considered intractable can now be treated quite effectively. Although these gains have been significant and even lifesaving, there has historically been a lack of attention paid to the other side of the coin, namely our own happiness and the study of well-being. Indeed, we all know intuitively that happiness is something far beyond the mere absence of misery. And yet, little attention has typically been paid to happiness as opposed to its opposite.

Nevertheless, a handful of researchers and practitioners over the years have attempted to look at related issues such as wellness, contentment, and thriving. For example, the psychologist Abraham Maslow promoted concepts such as "peak performances" and "self-actualization" to discuss what happens when people advance beyond mere survival and achieve their full potential. Similarly, the psychologist Carl Rogers spoke of the importance of achieving "full-functioning" and underscored the importance of helping people achieve the "good life." Others, too, have attempted to move beyond a disease-focused model of emotional health and uncover the secrets of the happy and meaningful life.

The past decade has witnessed a tremendous boom both within the mainstream and in academia. It seems like everywhere you look, there are magazines, books, and websites dedicated to helping people live happier and healthier lives. Pop psychology has indeed become big business. Conversely, within academic circles, happiness is no longer considered a silly or frivolous area of interest, and in fact has become a "hot topic" of research in recent years. We now know more about how to boost happiness and well-being than at any point in our history. Unfortunately, both academic psychology and the modern self-help movement possess notable drawbacks that counteract their considerable strengths.

BRIDGING THE DIVIDE

One of the great achievements of the modern self-help movement has been its ability to effectively reach millions of consumers, and to provide practical and concrete strategies to boost our happiness and psychological well-being. Unfortunately, its greatest weakness has been its overall lack of scientific rigor.

Indeed, many of the self-help approaches that you might come across have little if any scientific support (Norcross, 2000). Oftentimes, their message can be effectively distilled to: "This worked for me, so it'll work for you."

In fact, some of these approaches are likely to be helpful, but much more research needs to be done in order to say with any authority that they are effective. The realm of academia and professional psychology has a different sort of problem. The past ten to 15 years has seen an explosion of research regarding happiness and how to increase it. Best of all, these findings have been grounded in science such that we can truly have an understanding of what helps increase our happiness, and what doesn't. Unfortunately, much of academic psychology remains insulated from the world at large. Few, if any, of these findings trickle down to the public.

As a friend of mine who works in academic medicine jokingly laments, he can practically count on one hand the number of people who read his journal articles, and that number includes his mother! One of the primary aims of this book therefore is to help bridge that gap, and to bring you the very best of what the science of happiness has to offer. Best of all, we will be introducing concrete and easy-to-use strategies to help boost your happiness, backed by mounds of scientific evidence.

HAPPINESS OVERLOAD

Have you ever tried looking for some product at a store and been greeted with dozens or even hundreds of similar products that all look pretty much the same? It can be overwhelming and often feels akin to finding a needle in a haystack. Seeking answers when it comes to happiness can feel much the same. We are inundated with books, websites, diets, and blogs, all promising to deliver happiness to us in a neat package. At the time of this writing, a Google® search for "how to be happier" results in over 90 million hits and counting. An Amazon.com® search for books on happiness generates thousands of results. As a happiness seeker, the choices can be downright daunting. Discovering truths about happiness and well-being in this ocean of information can feel like trying to find a masterpiece within the biblical Library of Babel.

As discussed earlier, we know more about happiness and psychological well-being today than at any point in human history. For the first time, we possess a clear understanding of what sorts of strategies work in order to effectively boost our happiness, and which ones we can discard. And rather than relying on testimonials and theory alone, we can rely on science and allow it to guide us towards greater contentment, peace, and joy. The primary aim of this book is to help teach you some of these skills, in order to help guide you towards greater happiness and well-being in your own life.

THE BENEFITS OF BEING HAPPY

If you were to reflect on one change you could make in order to possibly extend your lifespan, what might it be? Would it be to quit smoking, or maybe cut down on your alcohol use? Perhaps you thought to reduce your red meat intake, or to commit to an exercise regimen. Each of these ideas would undoubtedly be a good place to start. But did any of you reading this come up with "being happier" as your chosen path towards a longer life?

We all know from our own experience that happiness is a good thing in and of itself. As we outlined earlier, it's at the very top of most people's list in terms of what they want most out of life. Studies show that most of us think about our own happiness and how to increase it at least once per day (Freedman, 1978). Here in the United States, our very own Declaration of Independence refers to the "pursuit of happiness" as one of our unalienable rights, along with life and liberty. Whether on a conscious or unconscious level, most of our major life decisions are made with the goal of maximizing our happiness.

Being happy is clearly a desirable state on an emotional level, and it undoubtedly feels good. But one of the most exciting findings in recent years is that this benefit of happiness is merely the tip of the iceberg. In fact, the more we learn about happiness and well-being, the more we understand just how crucial it is across a wide range of areas in our lives.

By increasing our happiness in a meaningful way, we can benefit our health, our relationships, our job performance, our emotional well-being, and even our bank account, in dramatic and life-altering ways. Furthermore, research shows that happy people live longer, have better marriages, are more creative, and are more altruistic than those who are less happy. In short, happiness doesn't just feel good to us. It's good *for* us too. In the next few brief sections, we'll review some of these key findings, and discuss their implications in our own lives.

SUNDAY SCHOOL REVISITED: LESSONS FROM NUNS

Between 1931 and 1943, a group of nuns entering convents in Milwaukee and Baltimore were asked to write brief autobiographical statements describing their lives and discussing their feelings about joining their religious order.

Some of the nuns wrote very practical, matter-of-fact letters outlining their lives to that point and their hopes in joining the order. For example, one of the letters went as follows: "I was born in 1909, the eldest of seven children. My candidate year was spent in the motherhouse, teaching chemistry. With God's grace, I intend to do my best for our order, for the spread of religion, and for my personal sanctification."

Contrast the words above with another letter written by a different nun, which read: "God started my life off well by bestowing upon me a grace of inestimable value. The past year which I have spent as a candidate studying at Notre Dame College has been a very happy one. Now I look forward with eager joy to receiving the Holy habit of Our Lady and to a life of union with Love Divine." Compared to the first letter, the second letter is filled with expressions of happiness, joy and positive affect. If you were to attempt to conjure an image of what these two nuns might be like in person, you might even able to get a sense of their personalities simply through these brief statements.

Two researchers, Deborah Danner and David Snowden, were intrigued by these differences and decided to investigate the link between the types of letters written by these nuns and their longevity. To do so, they sifted through 180 of these letters and coded them according to their level of *language positivity*. For example, letters that contained words such as "happy," "joyful," "grateful," or "love" were considered quite positive, whereas letters marked by an absence of these terms were rated as less positive. Danner and Snowden then divided the letters into quartiles, ranging from the happiest 25% to the least happy 25%. Finally, they attempted to determine whether there was in fact a connection between the degree of happiness expressed in a nun's letter and her longevity. As with the "Yearbook Study" discussed earlier, these researchers were pleasantly surprised, perhaps even shocked, by the results they discovered in the now-famous "nun study."

When they analyzed their data, Danner and Snowden discovered that those nuns in the top quartile in terms of happiness lived an average of *10 years* longer than those in the lowest quartile. Equally impressive, more than half of the most cheerful nuns were still alive at the age of 93, compared to a mere 18% of those in the least happy quartile. What makes these findings all the more compelling is the fact that these nuns proved to be remarkably excellent research subjects. For example, we know that they lived in the same towns, breathed the same air, ate the same food, and lived roughly the same lifestyle as one another. We are thus left with the likelihood that their level of expressed emotion, or happiness in this case, was directly connected to their respective lifespans.

Think that there's something special about nuns, or that these findings wouldn't hold true across a different sort of profession altogether? Another researcher, Sarah Pressman, decided to examine autobiographies of individuals from a very different line of work: Ninety-six of the most well-known psychologists. Similar to the "nun study," Pressman organized and coded these autobiographies according to their level of overall expressed happiness and language positivity. She discovered that those psychologists whose life stories were deemed most positive and happy lived an average of six years longer than their counterparts on the whole, whereas those whose writing was marked more by pessimism and negativity had lifespans five years shorter than average. So if you end up ever deciding to write an autobiography, be sure to include lots of happy memories!

HAPPINESS: GOOD FOR OUR MINDS

Think about a time when you've felt an intense negative emotion, whether it was anger, fear, or sadness. Can you remember where you were, whom you were with, and what you were doing? More importantly, can you recall how that particular emotion impacted your focus, your awareness, and your behaviors?

Negative emotions prompt narrow, immediate, and survival-oriented behaviors in our lives. As an example, think of the "fight or flight" response we experience when we feel intense anxiety or fear. Our focus narrows, we perceive threats more acutely, and our mind and body go on high alert. We zero in on the threats immediately in front of us, and our attention and efforts serve to aid in our immediate survival.

Positive and pleasant emotions have the opposite function in our lives. As the psychologist Barbara Fredrickson points out, positive emotions serve to "broaden and build" our personal resources. We seek out novel experiences, think in more creative ways, and demonstrate more interest and curiosity in new activities. When we are happy, we become receptive to a wide range of ideas, experiences, and ways of problem-solving far beyond our baseline. Our social circles broaden, we develop new skills and interests, and we achieve success in both life and love. Studies further show that when we encounter challenges in our lives, we tend to utilize significantly more creative and proactive styles of coping when we are in a positive mood compared to a negative one.

From a mental health perspective, there is now substantial evidence to suggest that positive emotions and happiness allow us to respond better to stress and adversity, and even help us become more resilient in the face of trauma (Tugade & Fredrickson, 2004). Furthermore, positive emotions serve to undo the effects of negative emotions on an emotional and even a physiological level (Frederickson, 2000).

Finally, it should be noted that through cultivating positive emotions and building happiness in our lives, we become buffered against future bouts of depression and low mood. Consider for a moment the way in which painful emotions have a tendency to feed off themselves and create a "downward spiral." Take the example of depression, in which our low mood leads us to withdraw from our normal activities, pull away from social support, and think negatively about others and ourselves. This in turn deepens our depressed mood even further, thus strengthening the cycle.

Positive emotions act in the opposite way. We seek out meaningful experiences, strengthen our social bonds while forging new ones, and engage in proactive problem-solving in the face of stress. Moreover, this cycle has a way of feeding on itself as well, creating what Frederickson refers to as an "upward spiral" of well-being.

HAPPINESS: GOOD FOR OUR HEALTH

We all want to lead long, healthy lives and many of the decisions we make are done in the service of becoming healthier and living longer. As mentioned earlier, we might cut down on our red meat or alcohol, exercise more or eat more fruits and vegetables in the hopes that doing so might improve our quality of life, our health, and our lifespan. As we learned from our nuns and baseball players earlier in this chapter, being happy not only feels good, it can help us live longer lives. In fact, subsequent research on happiness has shown that being happy can help increase our life expectancy by at least *nine years* (Emmons, 2007).

Aside from increased longevity, numerous studies have demonstrated via objective measures of health that happier people tend to become less sick, and have better immune system functioning than those who are more pessimistic (Dillon et al., 1985; Stone et al., 1994. As the psychologist Ed Diener points out, it's not simply that happier people *feel* healthier, they *are* in fact healthier.

One study that tracked participants over a thirty-year period found that the happiest participants were far less likely to experience problems including heart disease, high blood pressure, drug and alcohol dependence, and liver disease. Why might this be? Take the example of heart disease. Although diet, genetics, and exercise habits all play a significant role, emotional issues are one of the strongest predictors of subsequent heart problems. Specifically, a strong link has been shown between heart disease and depression, anger, and stress. By actively cultivating our own happiness, we can combat these negative emotional states and even buffer ourselves against physical health problems like the ones outlined above.

HAPPINESS: GOOD FOR OUR LIVES

In the "yearbook study" discussed earlier, we learned about some of the long-term benefits of being happy including greater likelihood of getting married and remaining married. Subsequent research has backed up these findings, and even shed light on some other surprising advantages of being happy.

From an interpersonal standpoint, happy people are more likely to describe their friendships as meaningful, and are more likely to report having a wide network of friends. It also turns out that many of the stereotypes of happy people, such as being self-centered or shallow, are dead wrong. On the contrary, happy people tend to be more cooperative, prosocial, and altruistic than those who are less happy overall (Williams & Shaw, 1999). Combined with the benefits to our romantic relationships discussed earlier, it becomes clear that being happy can enrich our lives from an interpersonal standpoint.

You may be wondering about success in the work place, since it stands to reason that having a bit of an "edge" could help in this regard. It's easy to envision happier people perhaps not being as invested at work and not pushing that extra mile towards success. But do "happy guys finish last," to borrow an old phrase? Absolutely not. Again, the research in this area suggests that the opposite is in fact true. As Ed Diener points out, a study of college freshmen demonstrated that those who were happy ended up making more money over a decade later, even after accounting for any initial wealth differences. Robert Emmons (Emmons, 2007) has further described how people who were rated "most cheerful" on an assessment of happiness ended up making an average of $25,000 more per year than those on the other end of the spectrum. So it indeed pays to be happy, not just figuratively, but literally as well!

CAN WE BECOME LASTINGLY HAPPIER?

As the findings discussed in this chapter illustrate, happiness is indeed worth cultivating and pursuing. We know from our own experience that being happy feels good and is inherently a good thing, and that building happiness is a worthwhile pursuit for its own sake. All of this, however, begs the question: Can we truly increase our overall happiness level, and can we do so in a meaningful and lasting way? The short answer to this question is a resounding *yes*. We can indeed boost our happiness level, and we can do it in ways that are not short-lived and fleeting but rather deep and enduring. Through the methods presented to you in this book, you will achieve a greater degree of positive emotions in your life, a sense of connection to the people around you and to your activities, and an increased sense of meaning and purpose.

In the chapters to come, you will learn about seven happiness-boosting principles that have been shown to lastingly increase our emotional well-being. They are:

- Cultivating Gratitude
- Kindness and Compassion
- Living in the Present Moment
- Fostering Self-Compassion
- Boosting Optimism
- Strengthening Relationships
- Practicing Forgiveness

Roadblocks to Well-Being

*"The greater part of our happiness or misery depends upon
our dispositions, and not upon our circumstances."*

—Martha Washington, former First Lady

THE HIGH PRICE OF WINNING

It should have been the happiest day of Billy Bob Harrell's life. The year was 1997, and Harrell was living paycheck-to-paycheck, struggling to make ends meet. A series of low-wage jobs, the most recent of which was at a home improvement store, had left him with barely enough money to live on after accounting for his monthly child support payments to his ex-wife. On his way home from work one evening, Harrell stopped to purchase some gas and a snack. As he was paying the clerk, he couldn't help but notice a sign nearby advertising the Texas State lottery, for which the prize had recently swelled to a whopping 31 million dollars. Harrell paid for his gas, paused briefly, and decided to buy a ticket. His life would forever be changed.

A few weeks later, Harrell was at home after another exhausting day at work. Relaxing in his favorite chair, he sat reading the local newspaper when he glanced down at the winning lottery numbers. Scrutinizing them, he compared them to the receipt from the ticket he had purchased. Slowly, it began to dawn on him that the impossible had happened. Indeed, Billy Bob Harrell held in his hand the winning ticket in the Texas State lottery. As the sole winner, he had just become 31 million dollars richer.

At first, it seemed as if all of his prayers had been answered. Previously in debt and struggling financially, Harrell now had enough money to live comfortably for the rest of his life. As his first order of business, Harrell quit his job, purchased a new car, and treated his family to a lengthy trip to Hawaii. A generous man, he donated large sums of money to various charities and to his church, and gave lavish gifts to friends. For a brief time, it seemed as if all of Billy Bob Harrell's problems had vanished, and his future seemed bright.

But the good times would soon turn into a nightmare. So-called friends and distant relatives came out of the woodwork, seeking a slice of Harrell's fortune. Even complete strangers began asking for handouts. In an effort to escape, Harrell tried changing his telephone number and moving out of town, to no avail. A series of financial blunders compounded his difficulties, and his life continued to spiral out of control. Less than a year after winning one of the largest prizes in lottery history, Billy Bob Harrell disclosed to a friend that he felt as if winning the lottery had been "the worst thing that ever happened" to him.

Things took an even more painful turn when his wife left him. By May of 1999, less than two years after winning the Texas State lottery, Harrell was broke and in debt. One evening, his son stopped by his house to check on him, and found Harrell lying dead in his home. The cause of death: a self-inflicted gunshot wound to the head.

****

The tragic tale of Billy Bob Harrell provides a cautionary reminder regarding our happiness. Here was a man who had experienced the sort of financial windfall that most of us can only dream of, and yet ended up in such misery that he took his own life shortly thereafter. If 31 million dollars can't make us happy, what will?

While most of this book will be spent discussing what we can do to lastingly increase our well-being and build greater happiness within ourselves, it is also crucial to understand how and why we often struggle to achieve this goal. As it turns out, there are a number of factors that impede our ability to be lastingly happy. Some of these have to do with our genes, while others pertain more to our patterns of thinking or even the world around us. But all told, they stand as roadblocks to our ultimate goal. Simply put, this chapter sheds light on a simple but often perplexing question: Why is it often so hard to be happy?

OUR QUEST FOR HAPPINESS

Have you ever daydreamed about owning a bigger house, purchasing a shiny new car, or looking younger and more beautiful? Perhaps you've caught yourself wishing to be free of physical pain, having more money in your bank account, or having a different boss. If you've dreamt of any of these sorts of changes in your life, chances are you yearned for them for a very simple and specific reason: You believed that achieving these dreams would make you happier.

Reflect for a moment on what you believe might make you happier. If you could change one thing in order to achieve greater mental and emotional well-being, what might it be? Close your eyes if you'd like, and imagine some future version of yourself, happy and fulfilled. What do you think might have to occur to help you get there? If you're like most people, you might have come up with answers such as:

- Finding a new job
- Moving to a new city
- Meeting the love of your life
- Achieving financial security
- Having children
- Owning a beautiful home
- Being more physically attractive
- Improving your physical health

This line of thinking is very common, and is often the first place we look towards when it comes to becoming happier. I call it the "If/Then" style of happiness thinking, and it tends to promote the idea that *if* we achieve a certain change in our life, *then* we will be happy. For example, we might tell ourselves that *if* we were to purchase that beautiful new house that came on the market, *then* we would achieve lasting happiness. Or *if* we were to have more financial security, *then* we would be content with our lives.

We all fall victim to this way of thinking from time to time. When I was a graduate student, I lived in a tiny apartment, routinely studied into the late hours of the night, and ate a diet that consisted of entirely too much McDonald's and ramen noodles. I was convinced that *if* I could just get through graduate school and get a real job, *then* I would finally be happy! Sure enough, when I finished school and received my first paycheck, I certainly felt happy...for a time. But unfortunately, this sort of happiness was fleeting and didn't last, for reasons we will explore later in this chapter.

The "If/Then" style of thinking is certainly seductive when it comes to happiness, but as we all know from personal experience it rarely leads to true and lasting well-being. The unfortunate truth is that none of the things listed earlier, including striking it rich, buying a new home, or moving to a different city, will lastingly change your happiness for the better. On the contrary, our pursuit of these sorts of goals often leads us astray, and pulls us away from the things that matter most in our lives.

Does this mean that the aim of this book, to help you become happier, is impractical and unfeasible? Absolutely not. However, it does mean that we often look for happiness in all the wrong places, and our attachment to this way of thinking about happiness is in fact one of our greatest sources of *unhappiness*. As Harvard psychologist and prominent happiness researcher Daniel Gilbert has aptly pointed out, most of us tend to be quite poor at predicting what will actually make us happy and fulfilled (Gilbert, 2006). As such, we often find ourselves working towards goals and pursuits that actually pull us away from lasting happiness and well-being.

OUR ENVIRONMENT: A NON-FACTOR IN HAPPINESS?

On a recent trip back home to New York, I had the good fortune of visiting the Tenement Museum located on the Lower East Side of Manhattan. This remarkable little nugget of New York history shows what life was like for the immigrants who settled in New York at the turn of the twentieth century. It was an eye-opening experience, both for the inspiring stories of perseverance and courage displayed by so many immigrants, but also for how different life was back then compared with today.

Like many of you reading this book, I've grown accustomed to many of the comforts inherent in today's world, such as central heating, television, and microwave ovens. But to the people living in the tenements, even things like running water and working plumbing were considered luxuries. Large families crammed into tiny apartments, often sharing beds with one another. For many, day-to-day life was a profound struggle.

The wealth and comforts of today's world would have seemed incredible to the immigrants living in the tenement buildings. And their experience was not unique; indeed, many Americans during those years had to go without running water and even without electricity. There were no flat-screen televisions, smartphones, or tablets. But were they doomed to be unhappy? Apparently not. In fact, Americans on average reported feeling slightly happier and more satisfied with their lives 75 years ago as compared to today (Lane, 2000).

Our environment and the circumstances around us play an odd and frequently frustrating role in terms of our happiness. While achieving our dream home, car, or job may lead to some initial euphoria, these efforts tend to make only small and fleeting differences in the long run. How small and fleeting? To illustrate, let's take a closer look at a few of the most common things that many of us pursue in our quest for happiness: money, marriage, physical attractiveness, and where we live.

Money and Wealth

Billy Bob Harrell's demise certainly showed some of the pitfalls faced by lottery winners, but a single anecdote doesn't tell the whole picture when it comes to the relationship between money and well-being. Fortunately, this link has been one of the most studied and scrutinized factors in the happiness research and some of the findings are quite eye-opening.

It's been said that money is the root of all evil. This is undoubtedly an exaggeration, but it's certainly safe to say that money is not the root of all happiness. We expect that more money will lead to greater well-being, but the research on happiness and well-being shows a far more nuanced picture. It is indeed true that for individuals who are below the poverty line and struggling to make ends meet, even a modest financial gain can yield substantial boosts in terms of well-being. And many studies also show that personal happiness levels tend to be higher in countries possessing greater material wealth and higher average incomes.

Despite these findings however, it appears that money and wealth has only a small overall impact on happiness once you reach a certain threshold, with the effect diminishing as you move up the ladder. One famous analysis by Nobel Prize-winning psychologist Daniel Kahneman suggests that the impact of money on happiness ceases to be significant once a person reaches an annual income of around $75,000 per year (Kahneman, 2010). Moreover, once a person has their basic needs met, such as food, clothing, and shelter, additional income beyond that point has only a marginal impact on well-being levels. To wit, another well-known study examining the happiness levels of the very wealthiest Americans showed that their personal happiness barely surpassed that of their own office staff and blue-collar workers (Diener et al., 1985).

These findings are surprising at first glance, but they help explain why overall levels of happiness and life satisfaction have stagnated (or perhaps even receded) in many developed nations. The emphasis on wealth, despite its miniscule impact on happiness past a certain point, helps shed light on why Americans feel no happier today than they did prior to World War 2 despite the immense material gains achieved over that time. Not only that, but it appears that our preoccupation with wealth may even have a detrimental effect on happiness.

In fact, one study on the connection between materialism and happiness found that individuals who listed "making money" as their main goal in life tended to do worse mentally and psychologically overall, with lower than average rates of happiness (Nickerson et al., 2003). Conversely, as we discussed briefly in the first chapter, one of the best ways to make more money is to become happier (Diener, 2008) with added wealth often coming as a byproduct. So while we may think that more money will make us happier, it turns out that we might have that connection backwards.

Marriage

Along with financial security, getting married is one of the other core pillars of the good life according to conventional wisdom. But much like wealth, the connection between marriage and happiness is a complex one. For many years, research suggested that married people tended to be happier, and that marriage was therefore a positive factor in terms of boosting emotional well-being. But these findings merely showed *correlation* rather than *causation*; in other words, they did not show whether or not getting marriage actually led to greater happiness, but rather showed that people who were married were more likely to report being happier.

So researchers were stuck with a bit of a "chicken and the egg" dilemma regarding marriage and happiness. Further research confirmed that while married individuals tended to be slightly happier overall with greater levels of well-being, the original scientists had it backwards. It now appears that happier people tend to be more likely to get married rather than vice versa. In other words, people who are happier tend to have stronger interpersonal connections, are more likely to enter into relationships, and are more likely to see those relationships flourish into marriages.

As for the causal effect of marriage on personal happiness, the data are less encouraging overall. It does appear that for most people, getting married does in fact lead to an initial boost in happiness that usually lasts around two years (Lucas et al., 2003). However, after that point, people tend to revert back to their previous levels of happiness. Overall then, it can be said that being married has only a *small* effect on a person's happiness when averaged across the various studies that have been done on the subject.

If these findings don't quite match with your own personal experiences, there may be a reason for that too. When I dug a little deeper on the topic, it does appear that the relationship between marriage and happiness is actually even more complex than first meets the eye. When marriage is looked at on a "macro-level," across thousands of couples that have been studied, it does indeed have only a small impact on happiness. And for the majority of people, marriage doesn't have a strong impact on their overall happiness level.

But on a "micro-level," the impact can be tremendous. In other words, an exceptionally happy and strong marriage can have a *huge* effect on an individual person's overall level of well-being, while an unhappy marriage can drastically contribute to one's misery. So while on average marriage has only a small impact, on either extreme its contribution to happiness can be substantial. Perhaps George Washington was correct then when he described marriage as either the "foundation of happiness or misery."

Physical Attractiveness

Everywhere we look, we are inundated with advertisements and messages in the media telling us about the latest beauty product, or the newest weight-loss procedure that will surely unlock the key to our lasting happiness. As an extreme example of our culture's obsession with appearance, look no further than the immense popularity of procedures aimed to make us look younger, thinner, or more attractive. Botox, liposuction, breast enhancements, hair transplants, plastic surgery...the list goes on and on. One would think, given the popularity of these procedures, that physical appearance must have an immense impact on happiness. But is this assumption correct?

While we might expect that positive changes to our appearance would indeed make us lastingly happier, extensive research on happiness suggests otherwise. Indeed, while most people are actually quite satisfied with their results from the various procedures listed above, as we have seen with money and marriage, any changes in overall happiness levels is likely to be fleeting and temporary. (Wengle, 1986).

But putting aside those who undergo cosmetic procedures for a moment, we might wonder whether individuals who are naturally quite attractive are any happier than the average person. Again, the answer appears to be no. In a series of studies conducted by psychologist Ed Diener, both happy and unhappy participants were blindly rated by judges according to level of attractiveness. Interestingly, there was no correlation found between the happiness levels of those who were rated as attractive compared to those who were rated as less handsome or beautiful (Diener, 1995).

A later study built on these findings and decided to examine people who make a living on their physical appearance: fashion models. Despite being blessed with naturally good looks, researchers found that models actually report much lower levels of happiness than the average person (Meyer, 2007). Interestingly however, there does seem to be one link between physical attractiveness and happiness:

Namely, happier people tend to rate themselves as more beautiful and attractive. So if you want to change how you feel about your appearance, don't waste time or money on cosmetic procedures. Instead, commit yourself to becoming happier!

Geography

Growing up in New York, I often dreamed of living in a more temperate climate. Summers were sweltering hot, and winters chillingly cold. Each winter, I can distinctly recall looking outside at the snow and thinking about how much happier I would be if I could just wake up to sunshine and warmth! Sure enough, I now live in one of the mildest climates in the world here in the San Francisco Bay Area. But while I'd like to think my change in geography and climate contributes to my happiness, the evidence for this is actually pretty weak. In one well-known study, a team of researchers asked participants in California and the Midwest to rate their happiness levels (Schkade & Kahneman, 1998). They found that although most participants *expected* that people living in California were happier, the results showed no differences between the two groups. Bad news for those of us out here in California, and good news for everyone else!

Summing Up

Changing our circumstances is often the first place we look in order to become happier. Whether it's earning more money, entering a relationship, having children, or buying a house, we often make decisions of this sort in our lives in the hopes of becoming happier. But time after time, we end up disappointed when our expected "happiness payoff" doesn't come to fruition.

How small of an impact do circumstances and environment have in terms of our happiness level? According to many studies, a mere *10 percent*. (Diener, 1999; Lyubomirsky, 2007). We expect that changes to our circumstances will unlock the key to joy and fulfillment, but this is rarely the case. It's not that these sorts of changes *don't* make us happier, because they often do. But they tend to make us a little bit happier, rather than a great deal happier. And that boost in happiness tends to last a short while, rather than a long time. This fact, perhaps more so than any other, accounts for how badly we miss the mark in terms of forecasting our own happiness.

This concept, that circumstances play a surprisingly small role in our happiness, is perhaps best summed up by Daniel Kahneman (1998), who explains that:

> People are exposed to many messages that encourage them to believe
> that a change of weight, scent, hair color (or coverage), car, clothes,

or many other aspects will produce a marked improvement in their happiness. Our research suggests a moral, and a warning: Nothing that you focus on will make as much difference as you think.

But why, exactly, do changes in our circumstances or environment yield such a small and temporary boost in our happiness?

HEDONIC ADAPTATION: GRAVITY FOR HAPPINESS

When I arrived on campus for my freshman year of college in New York, I remember being delighted to learn that my dormitory would be located right on Broadway, within walking distance of countless restaurants, bars, and shops. But being so close to the action had its downsides, as I learned my first night sleeping there. As soon as I turned off the lights to try and fall asleep, I was barraged by honking cars and people yelling, continuing all through the night.

I didn't sleep a wink that first night. Or the second night. In fact, for the first few weeks I had a difficult time getting much rest at all due to the noise level. And then something peculiar happened. Without realizing it, I suddenly got used to all the commotion and racket. Before long, I was sleeping like a baby, and the sounds streaming in from outside didn't bother me at all. In fact, when I would later move out to California (in a much quieter neighborhood), I had a difficult time adjusting to how quiet things were and even missed all those honking cars!

Human beings have a remarkable capacity to adapt to changes in our surroundings. This is perhaps best illustrated by the way in which we adjust to physical changes around us. For example, think about how your eyes adjust to the low light in a movie theater, or how an unpleasant odor ceases to be noticeable once you've adjusted to it for a little while. From a physical standpoint, our body tends to revert to a place of equilibrium, or homeostasis. The examples listed above constitute a process called *physiological adaptation*, and refers to our ability to adapt to physiological changes in our environment.

As it turns out, a very similar process occurs when it comes to our well-being as well, and known as *hedonic adaptation*. Hedonic adaptation refers to the idea that we tend to revert back to our typical happiness baseline despite changes in our environment. It helps explain why even major life events may result in a temporary happiness boost only to dissipate shortly thereafter.

The process of hedonic adaptation is perhaps the single greatest reason why changes in our lives (like the ones we discussed in the last section) yield only short-term boosts to our happiness levels. Even major positive events seem to have only temporary boosts. Consider one famous study that looked at winners of the Illinois State Lottery (Brickman, 1978). After winning their prize, the lottery winners were initially quite happy. But less than a year later, they reported being no happier than the average person when asked about their happiness. In fact, some reported that they had become *less* able to enjoy simple, day-to-day pleasures as compared to before they won the lottery.

As you might imagine, lottery winners aren't the only ones vulnerable to the effects of hedonic adaptation. Indeed, we see the same exact pattern occur across any number of positive life events including marriage, getting a new job, entering a new relationship, or buying a new home. A similar pattern emerges in which people experience an initial boost to their happiness level, only to slowly but surely revert back to their previous baseline.

Why does this process occur? Research identifies two major sources for the phenomenon (Lyubomirsky, 2007). The first is *social comparison*, which refers to the fact that we tend to look to those around us as a litmus test of normalcy. As such, we compare ourselves to the people around us, so that when our neighbor buys a 64-inch flat screen television, we start to think we need one too. The second factor influencing hedonic adaptation is the fact that we have *rising aspirations*. When we become accustomed to a higher level of comfort or luxury, we tend to want even more. As an example, when I moved from my cramped studio apartment to a one-bedroom, I felt like I had struck gold. But before long, my one-bedroom apartment started to feel small as well! For these reasons, the British psychologist Michael Eysenck has likened our pursuit of happiness to being on a treadmill, where we find ourselves running faster and faster and yet remaining in the same place (Eysenck, 1990).

Is hedonic adaptation always a bad thing? Not necessarily. In fact, just as we fall back down to earth following positive life events, the same process actually works in the reverse following negative life events. Indeed, research shows that we have a tremendous ability to bounce back from setbacks across a range of settings in our lives, including our relationships, our health, our jobs, and more. Even in the most extreme circumstances, such as people struggling with end-stage renal disease, or accident victims losing the use of their legs, study after study shows that the painful toll of these experiences fade with time, far more quickly than people expect at the outset. In essence, we bounce back from bad experiences, but also fall back down from good ones, faster and more decisively than we anticipate.

So just as financial windfalls and strokes of good fortune fade with time, so too do the painful emotions associated with loss and setbacks. Like gravity pulling us back towards our baseline, hedonic adaptation serves as a powerful barrier to happiness. It reminds us that unless we actively do something to change our happiness baseline for the better, we will tend to revert back to what we know. We now turn our attention to another powerful barrier to happiness: our genes.

THE GENETIC LOTTERY

This is a true story about two men named Jim. Both were born and raised in Ohio, where they lived approximately 45 minutes apart but never met. Both Jims were married twice, and both happened to marry women named Linda and Betty. Both had children, including sons named James. Both of the Jims were avid dog lovers, and each had a dog named Troy. The two Jims each liked to unwind by having a beer, and both chain-smoked the same brand of cigarettes. There were the same height, weight, and build. They both drove Chevrolets, and both worked as deputy sheriffs in their respective hometowns. Their personalities, temperament, and intelligence levels were remarkably similar.

The story of the two Jims would be interesting enough, considering their amazing similarities and series of coincidences. But what makes their true tale all the more remarkable is the fact that the two Jims were not exactly complete strangers; they were actually related. In fact, they were identical twins raised apart since birth. Having never met, they were reunited years later as a result of a famous study on twins. Their similarities were shocking, and help highlight the immense power of genetics on our development.

The nature versus nurture debate permeates many areas of inquiry, including the field of happiness. As with most things, our personal happiness is derived from a combination of factors, with our genes playing a strong role in terms of our happiness and well-being. As the story of the two Jims illustrates, our genes play a crucial part in our temperament, personality, habits, and preferences. Although theirs is an extreme example, scientists have carefully examined the impact of genes on one's happiness and found that the impact is surprisingly large. Estimates vary, but the current consensus seems to be that genes account for as much as 50 percent of a person's happiness level (Lyubomirsky, 2007).

How did researchers arrive at this figure? Through a series of studies examining both fraternal and identical twins, which consistently found identical twins to be much more strongly correlated in terms of happiness than fraternal twins. Building on these findings, researchers then took things a step further, and studied the happiness levels of twins who had been separated at birth. They found that identical twins remained closely correlated in terms of happiness, even when raised in drastically different environments. The conclusion of these famous twin studies has been that our genes account for approximately half of our overall well-being level.

Have you ever known someone who seems to take setbacks in stride, and who tends to always see the glass as half full? Conversely, can you think of someone for whom being happy seems like a constant uphill struggle? Some people are indeed more "wired" or predisposed to be happy, and are blessed with dispositions making it easier for them to feel happy, optimistic, and content. Unfortunately, others among us are not so lucky, and tend to struggle more with feelings of pessimism and discontent.

Our genes play a strong role in determining our overall happiness "set point," which refers to our baseline level of happiness that we tend to revert to thanks to hedonic adaptation as we discussed in the last section. Think of it like weight: some of us may be naturally heavy or thin, and in the absence of proper diet or exercise we tend to drift towards wherever our genes point us. But this doesn't mean we are doomed to be a mere reflection of this genetic set-point, and we can transform ourselves based on the choices and behaviors we engage in.

Our happiness follows in much the same way. Though we cannot change our genes, we can certainly change how happy we are through the approaches outlined in this book. Fifty percent (or so) is a sizable influence that is accounted for by our genes. Nevertheless, a tremendous amount of our happiness remains under our control, and within our power to change.

WIRED TO BE UNHAPPY?

Have you ever felt as if a dozen good things can happen to you in a day, but the one bad or disappointing thing that you encounter is the one that stands out and sticks with you? Or that you find yourself continually dwelling on stressors or ruminating about the negative, while being unable to "stop and smell the roses"? You're not alone, and in fact we can thank another barrier to happiness for this phenomenon: our very own brain.

It may seem strange that a psychologist like myself would describe our brain as a barrier to happiness. However, it's worth remembering that the human brain developed in the interest of survival, not necessarily to feel happy. Our ancestors needed to pass on their genes in order for the species to go on. As such, our brains have developed over the millennia to become acutely focused on how to live another day and survive.

Life was difficult for early humans, with constant threats of famine, natural disaster, warfare, and harsh elements surrounding them at all times. In order to survive, we have become highly attuned to threats and danger, and to focus on the negative rather than the positive. Though our world has changed a great deal since those days, our brains haven't, and we are still operating with much of the same basic machinery that our ancestors did hundreds of thousands of years ago.

Our brains possess a built-in "negativity bias," which has been shown to exist both in the laboratory and in the real world. This means we remember bad outcomes much more easily than good ones, and negative events impact us much more strongly than positive ones. This negativity bias has been shown to be so strong in fact, that studies suggest we need to experience around five positive events just to overcome the impact of a single negative one.

The neuropsychologist and author Rick Hanson has described our brains as being like: "Velcro® for bad, and Teflon® for good." This means that the very traits that helped ensure survival of our species also make it hard for us to be happy (Hanson, 2009). Our brain's negativity bias leads us to feel unhappy and stressed much of the time, especially if we are not actively working on changing it. Fortunately, scientists have developed many methods for changing this tendency, which we will revisit and practice later in this book. In fact, a recurring theme throughout this book is the concept of *self-directed neuroplasticity*, which refers to the idea that we can actively change our brains through both our behaviors and mindset. We will even introduce habits and techniques to help activate certain parts of our brains associated with positive emotions, tranquility, and happiness.

THE IMPACT OF MODERN CULTURE

If you were to reflect on some of the most common societal messages we receive when it comes to our happiness, what comes to mind? If you live in the United States, or any Western nation for that matter, chances are a few ideas rise to the top. These tend to include things like wealth, youth, physical attractiveness, having a high number of friends, material possessions, and the like. As you've probably surmised by now, these share something in common: They have little if any impact on our happiness, though we often expect them to.

In contrast to the items above, we hear comparatively little about the things that actually make a tremendous impact on our happiness and well-being. Things like the transformative power of gratitude, the importance of slowing down and becoming present in the moment, and the benefits of forgiveness are often treated as afterthoughts in our world. And yet they are crucial for us to cultivate, in order to live a life of true fulfillment and happiness.

In many respects, we are living in an era of crisis when it comes to happiness and well-being. Despite the immense gains of the past century in terms of material wealth and comfort, individual happiness levels have stagnated and in many cases even declined. Mental illness is on the rise, with over a quarter of Americans struggling with diagnosable psychiatric illnesses including 15% suffering from depression (Kessler, 1994). Worse yet, these rates are on the rise, with severe depression being as much as ten times more common today than even fifty years ago (Seligman, 2002). One prominent thinker (Blazer, 2005) even went so far as to dub our current epoch as "The Age of Melancholy."

As I examine these and other trends, I can't help but wonder about the strong connection between our culture and our increased rates of misery. This isn't to suggest that all progress has been for naught, and indeed there are many immensely positive changes that have occurred as a result of modernization and development. But there is a dark underside to it as well, and one that can often pull us away from true happiness if we're not careful. When we become too drawn to societal messages regarding happiness, we lose time and energy that could be devoted to more meaningful pursuits.

My goal isn't to encourage you to stop shopping, cut off social media, and pass on buying the latest smartphone. I certainly will continue to do those things myself. But rather, it's to become aware of the ways in which these pursuits can, at times, pull you away from the things that matter most to you and that help foster true happiness in your life.

Misunderstanding True Happiness

A final barrier we face when it comes to creating a life of true happiness stems from our widespread misconception about what happiness really is. Considering it's something we all aspire to on some level, it is remarkable that the idea of happiness can mean so many different things to so many different people. In the first chapter we discussed how true happiness consists not only of positive emotions, but also a deeper sense of meaning, purpose and connection in our lives. Feeling good is undoubtedly important, but true happiness goes far beyond that.

We often confuse true happiness with the sort of happiness we see in the media or television, which I consider the "Hollywood" version of happiness. This notion of happiness is marked by strong positive emotions, with an absence of negative emotions or emotional pain. While it's important to have a sense of subjective well-being, how we feel in a given moment is often transient and is not the mark of true and deep happiness. Indeed, we need the second layer of happiness that consists of feeling that our lives are worthwhile and have meaning.

CAUSE FOR HOPE?

Given the many barriers to happiness that we've discussed in this chapter, you might find yourself feeling somewhat skeptical or even discouraged regarding the prospects of becoming happier. After all, we are up against a whole host of roadblocks including our genes, hedonic adaptation, our brains, and more.

But despite these factors, allow me to offer a different perspective. Now that you are equipped with the knowledge of what makes happiness so difficult, you are empowered to choose something different. Rather than seek happiness in all the wrong places (such as changing your circumstances), or feeling frustrated that your genetic set-point may be on the lower end, you have the power to invest your energy into something with the potential to be life-changing. Because in spite of all the factors that make it difficult to be happy, it is very much in your power to become significantly happier than you currently are. This book shows the way.

The Power to Change

"People are just as happy as they make up their minds to be."

—President Abraham Lincoln

MEANING FROM SUFFERING

It would be difficult to conjure up a more tragic and traumatic upbringing than the one experienced by Christina Noble. Born into one of the most impoverished neighborhoods of Dublin, Ireland, Noble's formative years were marked by ongoing loss and immense pain. Looking back on it today, she describes her upbringing as "the poorest of the poor." And things would only get worse.

When Christina was only ten years old, her mother passed away unexpectedly. To make matters worse, her father (a severe alcoholic) abruptly left the family as well, leaving Christina and her younger siblings to fend for themselves. They were soon scooped up by authorities and scattered off to various orphanages, separated at a young age. The formative years of her life were marked by misery, and her adolescence was no better. As a teen, Christina was gang-raped by four men who pulled her into a car and brutalized her.

Seeking to escape the endless chaos, she married a man who turned out to be an abusive alcoholic, and Christina was once again trapped and needing to escape. But escape she did, and despite the immense turmoil of her life Christina managed to persevere and rise above her challenges in order to build the type of legacy most of us would be in awe of. Today, Christina heads up the Christina Noble Foundation, a non-profit devoted to helping disadvantaged children around the world.

****

In the last chapter we discussed Billy Bob Harrell, a man whose tragic death exposes the myth that wealth and financial security is a key to happiness.

Here was a man who experienced the sort of financial boon that most people can only dream of, and yet ended up in such misery and despair that he took his own life. Conversely, Christina Noble was dealt a terrible hand in life and yet was able to build a life of meaning, joy, and service. Like a phoenix rising from the ashes, she overcame misfortune and pain in order to create a happy and meaningful life.

CAN WE TRULY BECOME HAPPIER?

Although many of our major decisions and life choices are made in the hopes of maximizing our happiness level, most of us tend to be quite poor at increasing our happiness in a lasting and meaningful way. For many, it can often feel like a constant struggle to achieve a sense of happiness and well-being. In the last chapter, we reviewed several of the most prominent barriers we face in the pursuit of happiness. These included obstacles such as hedonic adaptation, being born with a low genetic set-point, and even our brain's built-in "negativity bias." Because of these and other findings, it was long assumed that attempting to raise one's happiness was a fool's errand.

Fortunately, this pessimism has turned out to be unfounded, with countless studies now showing that it is indeed possible for us to become happier and for that happiness boost to last. The key is to shift our efforts away from the things that don't matter and towards the sorts of pursuits that do. We don't have to rely on being blessed with "good genes," or stumble upon strokes of luck or good fortune in order to be happy. Rather, it comes down to the choices we make, the behaviors we engage in, and the habits we cultivate. You, and no one else, hold the power to change.

HOW MUCH HAPPINESS IS UNDER OUR CONTROL?

Changing our genes isn't within our power, and changing the situations and circumstances around us provides little boost to our well-being. So where does that leave us? In short, it comes down to the choices we make, habits we create, and mindset we cultivate. These factors account for an estimated 40% or more of a person's happiness level (Lyubomirsky, 2008). If we stop and think about it, this is an absolutely huge amount that remains under our control, accounting for four times the influence of things like our bank account, our marital status, or our physical appearance.

We often get sidetracked and pulled towards things that have only a small effect on our happiness, despite our hopes to the contrary. By shifting our focus and efforts away from those sorts of fruitless endeavors, and taking the steps outlined in this book, you have the power to harness the vast potential within you to become happier, starting today.

WHAT SCIENCE CAN TEACH US

Interest in happiness and well-being has exploded over the past decade or so, with new books and magazines on the subject hitting the shelves at a blistering pace. Sometimes it feels as if each day brings a new diet, form of exercise, or approach that promises to deliver everlasting happiness to its adopters. The unfortunate reality is that most of the "latest and greatest" happiness approaches found in popular media have not been held up to scientific scrutiny. In many cases, their effects may dissipate quickly, or often hold no real benefits at all.

There are seemingly infinite ideas out there about what brings us happiness, from religious theories to "old wives' tales." In some cases, old wisdom or common sense has been proven right, but often times the science shows a surprisingly different story and helps to separate the wheat from the chaff, so to speak. I am not a researcher myself, and instead work clinically with patients both in a hospital setting as well as in my private practice. But I am a committed devotee of relying on science and research, rather than hearsay or intuition, to guide my work. By distilling the latest happiness research, and combining it with my own experience of working with patients on an everyday basis, I hope to provide you with a happiness-building program that is both evidence-based and also easy to implement and often fun to do.

THE IMPORTANCE OF FOLLOW-THROUGH

When I was younger, I remember watching an interview with the professional basketball star, Michael Jordan. Despite being blessed with immense physical gifts, he described instead the countless hours he would spend in the gym each day honing his craft. It was not enough to merely go through the motions, or to rest on his laurels. Rather, Jordan spoke to the importance of maintaining his skills each day, building on his areas of strength, and working on his areas of weakness.

Strange as it may sound, we must approach the task of building happiness and well-being with the same sort of purpose and tenacity. As you read this book, you'll be learning about a wide range of proven approaches shown to increase happiness. But merely reading this book won't be sufficient; rather, the most important thing is that you *complete* the exercises and *practice* the skills. It's crucial to continue to integrate them into your daily life in order to continue reaping their rewards.

Feeling intimidated or worried? Don't be! In my experience, most people who embark on this journey find it to be so self-reinforcing and rewarding that it doesn't end up feeling like "work." As with anything worth striving for though, building and maintaining greater happiness will take effort and energy. But by investing energy into your own happiness, the gifts you receive can be immense and life changing.

How to Use This Book

Starting in the next chapter, you'll be learning about seven principles, or paths, to happiness and well-being. Each path has been scientifically shown to increase happiness in a lasting and meaningful way. The next seven chapters can either be read in order or according to your interests and goals. For example, if you are wanting help in appreciating the good things more in your life, feel free to start with the chapter on gratitude. Conversely, if a grudge or resentment is holding you back and interfering with your happiness, you might choose to start with the chapter on forgiveness. Or of course, you might prefer to simply go in order, and that's OK too.

As for how much of the book to use, or how many exercises to complete, again the answer is flexible. Each of the next seven chapters can be viewed as either a standalone approach, or as part of a larger whole, depending on your goals and needs. But most people do find that they prefer to read through the entire program contained in this book, at whatever pace is most comfortable, and then focus on whichever skills and tools are most relevant for them. Part of that is because we oftentimes don't quite know which approaches or principles will be most helpful for a given person until we try them. So I encourage you to gradually work through each exercise with an open mind, in order to discover which ones end up being most helpful.

Along these lines, I encourage you to strike a balance between openness and skepticism while you read through this book. Think critically as you work through the material, and consider what will work for you as an individual. Consider the recommendations as a guide, able to be individualized based on your personality, schedule, style, and preferences. Indeed, the exercises and skills introduced in this book are based on scientific findings about what tends to be helpful for most people. But you are an individual, and as an individual some adjustments may be necessary and are indeed encouraged.

Finally, I cannot overstate the importance of not simply reading through the chapters, but also completing the exercises at the end of each chapter. Many of the exercises or techniques involve writing, and for these, I encourage you to use whatever means or materials are most comfortable. Some of you might enjoy purchasing a journal to use as a companion for this book, while others might prefer using a computer or tablet. There's no right or wrong way to complete the writing exercises, so I encourage you to use whatever feels most appropriate for you. The most important thing is that you begin practicing the skills, and integrating them into your day-to-day life.

The Path of Gratitude

"He is a wise man who does not grieve for the things which he has not, but rejoices for those which he has."

—Epictetus

INSPIRATIONAL GRATITUDE

On July 4, 1939, a sellout crowd of over sixty thousand fans at Yankee Stadium rose to their feet to cheer on their hero, legendary first baseman Lou Gehrig. For fourteen seasons, Gehrig had been a shining example of strength and excellence, setting a major league baseball record for consecutive games played and becoming one of the most feared hitters in all of baseball. The "Iron Horse," as he was known, was a tower of strength, a larger than life star whose on-field prowess was allegedly matched only by his generosity and good cheer.

Just a few months earlier, Gehrig had begun the season with the rest of his teammates, hoping to capture another championship. But it quickly became clear that something was terribly wrong. His coordination was failing him, and his speed had slowed. At one point, while running around the bases, Gehrig fell. On another occasion, he collapsed seemingly out of nowhere. The "Iron Horse" was simply not himself.

Extensive tests conducted by the Mayo Clinic determined that Lou Gehrig was indeed not well, and in June of 1939 he was diagnosed with Amyotrophic Lateral Sclerosis, or ALS as it is better known. His career was over, and his life was forever changed. Doctors gave Gehrig perhaps three years to live.

When Gehrig arrived at Yankee Stadium on Independence Day, he was greeted by deafening cheers and an extensive ceremony conducted in his honor. The New York Times described the scene as "perhaps as dramatic a pageant as ever was enacted on a baseball field." Noteworthy speakers that day ranged from the Mayor of New York, Fiorello La Guardia, to Gehrig's longtime teammate and occasional friendly rival, Babe Ruth. Each commented on Gehrig's strength and perseverance in the face of such adversity, and expressed admiration for his courage. Finally, despite his protestations due to his discomfort with the spotlight, it was Lou Gehrig's turn to address the crowd.

With stadium loudspeakers echoing his voice, the "Iron Horse" stood before the packed crowd and proceeded to count his blessings. He expressed thanks to the visiting New York Giants, his longtime rivals, for sending him gifts and kind words before the game. He expressed thanks to his teammates, managers and coaches who had shared in his journey. And despite all he was going through, and the bad hand he had been dealt, Gehrig stood before the crowd and exclaimed that he considered himself, "the luckiest man on the face of the earth." He concluded by stating that although he had been given a bad break, he still felt that he had "an awful lot to live for." For nearly two minutes, the crowd stood and cheered, and Lou Gehrig wiped tears from his eyes, thanking them.

****

We don't often think of gratitude as something that can transform our lives. In fact, we often don't think of gratitude much at all. In America in particular, gratitude is what social scientists refer to as a "hypocognized" emotion, meaning that we tend not to give it much thought nor appreciate it very much (Emmons, 2007). For some of us, our only formalized way of practicing gratitude occurs on our annual day of feasting on turkey and watching football each Thanksgiving.

And yet the cultivation of gratitude has been shown to be one of the most effective and reliable ways to boost our own happiness and to change our lives in meaningful and lasting ways. We don't need to have the strength and heroism of Lou Gehrig to reap the considerable rewards of gratitude. In fact, the most powerful ways to boost gratitude are often found in small ways, in our day-to-day existence. By harnessing gratitude and integrating it into our lives, we can become lastingly happier, healthier, and more effective in our lives. This chapter will show you just how powerful and life changing the practice of gratitude can be, and will teach you practical and effective ways to begin implementing it in your life, starting today.

WHAT IS GRATITUDE?

The world's foremost expert on gratitude, Robert Emmons, defines gratitude as "a sense of wonder, thankfulness, and appreciation for life." He goes on to describe gratitude as consisting of two separate but interconnected parts. First, it is acknowledging the goodness that is present in our lives. Second, it is a recognition that the source of these blessings lies at least partially outside of the self (Emmons, 2007). As Emmons points out, when we are grateful we "acknowledge that other people–or even higher powers, if you're of a spiritual mindset–gave us many gifts, big and small, to help us achieve the goodness in our lives."

Gratitude can exist as an external behavior, such as the act of thanking someone, but can also be a more private or internal process, such as acknowledging and reflecting on the good aspects of our life. It can often be tempting to attribute our success and good-fortune solely to our own efforts and hard work, and we can at times forget to stop and reflect on all that we have to be thankful for and the people who have helped us along the way. As Bart Simpson noted during an episode of *The Simpsons* while attempting to say grace, "Dear God, we paid for all this food ourselves, so thanks for nothing." However, we would be wise to follow the guidance of the ancient Chinese proverb that instructs us "when eating bamboo sprouts, remember the man who planted them." Indeed, when we can appreciate and savor the interpersonal aspects of our good fortune, our lives become all the more enriched.

WHY PRACTICE GRATITUDE?

The past decade has witnessed an explosion of exciting findings regarding the benefits of gratitude. As it turns out, gratitude is not only an emotion that feels good; it's been connected to a number of other psychological, physical, and social benefits as well. Happiness researcher Sonja Lyubomirsky describes gratitude as "an antidote to negative emotions, a neutralizer of envy, avarice, hostility, worry, and irritation." Other findings support the notion that the cultivation of gratitude is indeed one of the keys to boosting our happiness. Furthermore, people who are grateful report lower levels of depression, improved physical health, describe more meaningful interpersonal relationships, and are more compassionate and forgiving towards others.

You may be wondering whether these findings are merely correlational or if they are causal. In other words, is it simply a case that people who are less depressed, are in better physical health, and have better relationship have more to be grateful for, and therefore report feeling more grateful? Moreover, is gratitude a disposition that we are either blessed with or not, and is it possible to actually become more grateful? The answers to each of these questions are encouraging. Research shows that gratitude is actually a *causal* factor in the situations outlined above, meaning that when we practice gratitude more regularly we are more likely to have good things happen to us on both a psychological and social level (Lyubomirsky, 2007). In addition, studies further show that gratitude is something that can in fact be cultivated, practiced and worked on, no matter your starting point. Taken together, these findings suggest that not only *can* we become more grateful in our lives; we actually *should* because it's so good for us! By "wanting what we have" and integrating gratitude more into our lives, we can indeed transform our lives and lastingly boost our happiness level.

GRATITUDE: GOOD FOR OUR MINDS

Think about something that you feel grateful for at this current time. It can be something small, large, recent, or from far in the past. Take a moment if you need, and identify the source of your gratitude. Allow yourself to really get in touch with the emotions that come up for you. What other feelings come to mind when you reflect on it? If you're like many people, you may notice a sense of peace, tranquility, calmness, and contentedness. You are unlikely to describe feeling upset, stressed, or angry when you are reflecting on these feelings of gratitude. In this way, gratitude often serves as a sort of "gateway emotion," in that it tends to lead directly to other positive feelings and connectedness to the good aspects of our lives. As the Roman philosopher Cicero observed, "Gratitude is not only the greatest of virtues, but the parent of all the others."

The practice of gratitude has indeed been shown to lead to a wide range of mental health benefits. Sonja Lyubomirsky points out that gratitude has been strongly linked to many other positive emotional states including a higher volume of positive emotions, greater joy, and deriving more pleasure in our lives. Underscoring these points, gratitude researcher Robert Emmons discovered that people who regularly engaged in gratitude practice for ten weeks reported happiness increases over *twenty-five percent higher* than those in a control group. He further showed that those who practiced gratitude were more hopeful and optimistic about their future, and even reported feeling more enthusiastic and determined. Indeed, gratitude has been shown to be a powerful promoter of positive emotions, ranging from greater optimism and forgiveness, to increased happiness and life satisfaction.

But what if we are feeling depressed, or struggling with anxiety? Can the practice of gratitude help us then? Again, the results in this area appear to be quite promising. Studies show that gratitude may serve as a protective factor against episodes of depression, perhaps due to the fact that gratitude can "undo" many of the harmful thinking patterns present in individuals with depression. When we are depressed, we often tend to fixate on the negative aspects of our lives and engage in unhealthy rumination about these problems.

Conversely, there is an inherent strong inverse relationship between gratitude and depression, borne out in the research. Practicing and cultivating gratitude has been shown to lead to lower levels of depression and anxiety, and can even reduce the intensity and duration of episodes of depression (Wood, 2010). Studies conducted by Martin Seligman showed that a mere fifteen days of gratitude practice provided substantial relief for patients who had initially scored in the "severe" range of depression (Seligman et al, 2005). In fact, after this brief period of practice, over *ninety percent* reported experiencing relief and their scores dropped down to the "average" range for depressive symptoms.

If you've suffered significant trauma in your life, the practice of gratitude can be of service to you. In examining the course of PTSD in veterans of the Vietnam War, happiness researcher Todd Kashdan found that gratitude helped ameliorate the effects of trauma and aided in the healing process. Specifically, the findings suggested that greater levels of gratitude was linked to greater positive affect and increased self-esteem among trauma survivors (Kashdan, 2005).

So whether you want to help recover from depression or anxiety, or merely want to be a bit happier, gratitude can be a powerful tool in bettering your life. As the findings outlined above demonstrate, Woody Allen may have actually been correct when he asserted that, "Being happy is appreciating and liking what you have, instead of what you don't have." It turns out, however, that the benefits of practicing gratitude extend far beyond our emotional mind and our moods. It can also help with our physical health and our relationships.

GRATITUDE: GOOD FOR OUR BODIES

In a now-classic study on the power of gratitude, researcher Robert Emmons asked research participants to perform one of three tasks for a period of ten weeks. The first group of participants was asked to record, once each week, five things that they felt particularly grateful for that had occurred in the past week. The second group was asked to record five hassles or stressful things that had occurred during the past week. And the third group was instructed to simply write down five events, good or bad, that had occurred during the past week. All the while, these individuals were completing extensive journals and surveys, assessing themselves in a range of areas including mood, sleep, exercise habits, and more.

At the end of the ten-week experimental period, Emmons and his colleagues analyzed their data to see if any significant differences had emerged among the three experimental groups. They were pleasantly surprised by what they found. Not only did the practice of gratitude benefit participants from a mental health standpoint; it turned out to be hugely beneficial in terms of their physical health as well.

Compared to participants in the other two conditions, those in the gratitude group reported fewer health complaints and endorsed far fewer symptoms of physical illness overall. They exercised more; in fact, they reported exercising a full ninety minutes more per week than the participants who were asked to reflect on their daily hassles. Even their sleep improved, as subjects in the gratitude condition reported spending less time awake prior to falling asleep, and even described themselves as far more rested and refreshed the next morning.

A subsequent study by Alex Wood in 2009 suggests that by focusing on the good in our lives, the nature of our thoughts changes just before bedtime. Such a practice helps shift our attention away from anxieties and worries and can help promote more relaxation thus setting the stage for a better night's sleep. Considering the immense risks of poor sleep on our overall well-being, in terms of stress on our bodies along with greater risk of depression, this is indeed an exciting finding. We are often told to count sheep in order to help ourselves fall asleep. But according to this study, we may be better off counting our blessings in order to fall asleep more quickly, and feel more rested!

GRATITUDE: GOOD FOR OUR RELATIONSHIPS

I mentioned in the beginning of this chapter that the practice of gratitude is often quite interpersonal in nature because by definition, we are identifying blessings that have come our way from outside of our personal control. Often these come from the people around us, and through gratitude we are able to stop and appreciate the help we have received from others in our lives. Perhaps it is not surprising then that the cultivation of gratitude in our lives not only leads to emotional and physical benefits, but also can yield immense interpersonal gains as well.

This intuition has now been supported by numerous academic studies, with research demonstrating that the practice of gratitude helps in both strengthening our existing social relationships, as well as forging new ones (McCullough et al., 2002). Those who regularly engage in gratitude practice have been shown to be more outgoing, less lonely, and less likely to isolate. Furthermore, people who regularly practice gratitude have been shown to be more helpful and altruistic towards others, even when there is a personal cost to themselves (Bartlett, 2006). If you're married or in a relationship, there's good news as well: practicing gratitude, particularly in relation to your partner, has been shown to lead to significantly higher relationship satisfaction (Algoe, 2010; Lambert, 2010).

Gratitude can even help us become more forgiving towards others. Forgiveness expert Fred Luskin has described how people who regularly cultivate gratitude in their lives have been shown to be far more forgiving and better equipped to let go of resentments. Even among divorced couples, a group we might normally associate with much anger and resentment, the practice of gratitude has been shown to reduce antipathy and promote forgiveness (Rye, 2012). So whether you want to improve an existing relationship or cultivate a new one, it appears that regularly integrating gratitude into your life is one of the best methods of achieving this goal.

THIS IS YOUR BRAIN ON GRATITUDE

It may seem surprising that the practice of gratitude can yield so many benefits across so many domains of our lives. But a closer look at the brain-based aspects of gratitude provides some clues about its effectiveness and power to promote happiness. Something that's often forgotten is that our brains are quite malleable, and change depending on our environment, our behaviors, and even what we think about. The technical term for this phenomenon is *neuroplasticity*, which refers to the changes that occur in our brains as a result of these factors. One of the most exciting findings in the field of neuroscience has been the discovery that the behaviors we engage in, the foods we eat, and even the things we reflect on have a direct and measurable impact on our brains.

Gratitude leads to several brain-based changes that help provide clues about its helpfulness as a happiness-boosting tool. The first is that practicing gratitude appears to boost the amount of the neurotransmitter *serotonin* in our brains. Serotonin influences a number of our bodily functions and is considered to be strongly connected to our moods. Notably, low levels of serotonin are thought to contribute strongly to depression. We've all seen the advertisements on television about antidepressant medications, many of which tend to operate by increasing the availability of serotonin in our brains. Amazingly, by reflecting on positive things in our life and practicing gratitude regularly, we can actually increase the amount of serotonin in our brains thereby helping to combat depression.

In addition to serotonin, gratitude has also been linked to dopamine, considered the "feel good" neurotransmitter in our brains. Beyond feeling good, dopamine is also strongly connected to helping us to initiate behaviors and take action. Once we feel rewarded by something, we become more likely to repeat this very same behavior over time. This might explain why the practice of gratitude, which undoubtedly feels good to engage in, also becomes so "addicting" for many people over time.

Another key part of our brains associated with the practice of gratitude is a small area called the *hypothalamus*. Though slight in size, the hypothalamus is mighty in terms of its function, and it helps to moderate our sleep, our stress levels, and even our metabolism. Recent studies have linked gratitude with increased activity in the hypothalamus (Zahn et al., 2009). Recall for a moment the exciting findings discussed earlier in this chapter about the impact of gratitude on our sleep, our health, and even on our physical exercise patterns. Although these benefits seem unrelated to one another at first glance, perhaps this finding about the link between gratitude and hypothalamic activity may help explain why this simple practice of gratitude yields such tremendous and wide-ranging benefits in our lives.

Finally, the practice of gratitude may lead to changes in an area of our brains referred to as the left prefrontal cortex. This region of our brain is considered to be the center for positive emotions, including love, happiness, and compassion. Exciting findings have pointed to increased neural activity in this part of the brain in people who regularly practice gratitude. Many years ago, the influential psychologist Donald Hebb pointed out that, "Neurons that fire together wire together." By strengthening the neural connections in our prefrontal cortex, we may be literally helping to wire our brain for happiness!

HOW AND WHY DOES GRATITUDE WORK?

As the examples above demonstrate, the practice of gratitude can literally transform our mind, our health, and our lives. But how does gratitude work, and why is it so incredibly helpful? Although the reasons are many, a few stand out. First, practicing gratitude directly counteracts the effects of hedonic adaptation, which as you'll recall from Chapter 2 of this book can act as a sort of "gravity" against positive events in our lives and continually pulls us back towards our "happiness baseline." Rather than be on the prowl for the next best thing to give us a temporary happiness boost, practicing gratitude allows us to savor and appreciate the good things that are already in our lives.

A second way in which gratitude works is through counteracting the "bad stronger than good" bias in our brains. As neuropsychologist Rick Hansen points out in his book entitled *Buddha's Brain*, our brains are wired to be like Teflon® for good experiences, but Velcro® for bad. By practicing gratitude, we help counteract this tendency and are better equipped to "take in the good" in our lives.

Thirdly, practicing gratitude helps to undo the physical and psychological effects of negative emotions, and can help buffer us against their recurrence. Consider for a moment how difficult it is to simultaneously bask in feelings of gratitude, while also experiencing intense negative emotions such as anger, resentment, or jealousy. Such a state is almost impossible to create; such is the power of gratitude.

Finally, and perhaps most importantly, the practice of gratitude yields numerous social and interpersonal benefits. By cultivating gratitude, we strengthen our social bonds and open up avenues to create new ones. We become more inclined to give back to others and engage in altruistic acts. The interpersonal nature of gratitude helps promote and foster social connectivity, which is indeed one of the keys to happiness.

GRATITUDE DURING HARD TIMES

When times are good, it can be easy to count our blessings. Practicing gratitude during those times can help us to magnify the positive aspects of our lives for which we are thankful, and lead to even greater feelings of happiness and well-being. But what about when we face adversity, hardship, and heartache? Can gratitude help us then?

When reflecting on the importance of gratitude during hard times, perhaps no better example can be found than our very own celebration of Thanksgiving. For it was not during times of abundance and prosperity that our national day of giving thanks was founded; rather it came on the heels of an incredibly challenging period in our forefathers' history. Indeed, the first Thanksgiving holiday was held following a difficult year in which nearly half of the pilgrims at Plymouth Plantation had perished due to famine, disease, and harsh conditions. Despite these hardships, they recognized the importance of giving thanks for what they had, and that such a practice could strengthen them and provide hope for a better future. We would be wise to follow their lead in our own lives.

Although practicing gratitude may prove more challenging when times are tough, research has shown that doing so may in fact be especially important. As gratitude expert Robert Emmons points out, practicing gratitude when we face adversity is not only helpful, it is crucial. This doesn't necessarily mean that we feel thankful for the hardships we face, nor does it mean that gratitude comes easily during times of struggle. Practicing gratitude during such times does not discount whatever pain we may be experiencing, because pain is an inevitable and often even a valuable part of life. It simply means that we have the power to choose, each and every moment, how we want to view our lives and what we wish to focus on.

In his book entitled *Man's Search for Meaning*, psychologist Viktor Frankl describes how though much remains out of our control, one of the few things we do have control over is the "last of human freedoms – the ability to choose one's attitude in a given set of circumstances." The research on gratitude suggests that during hard times, it may be particularly important to foster this practice. Practicing gratitude enables us to feel hope when things are seemingly hopeless, inspires us when we are demoralized, and connects us to others when we feel alone.

When I think about gratitude in the face of adversity, I can't help but to reflect on a former patient of mine that we will call Brian. When I first met Brian, he was progressively losing his vision due to complications of diabetes. A formerly active man who enjoyed all things outdoors from fishing to biking, Brian had become increasingly depressed and despondent. When our work began, he had even felt suicidal because he believed his life was over, and that he had nothing to live for.

It was around Thanksgiving time when things began to change for Brian. He recounted to me how he spent Thanksgiving with his children and grandchildren, and had one of the best days he could remember in years. "I realized I still have so much to be thankful for," he exclaimed to me with excitement. He went on the tell me how he had gone fishing with his sons, and even though he could barely see, "it felt wonderful just to feel the sea breeze and feel that boat rocking."

Brian went on to learn Braille, connected with others who shared a similar struggle, and was able to make meaning from his suffering through gratitude. He told me in one of our sessions that he had decided to "stop focusing on what I don't have anymore, and start focusing on what I do have." On a personal level, when I'm having a bad day or feel myself stuck going down a road of negativity, I still reflect back on my sessions with Brian. Through his courage and perseverance, he taught me about the power of gratitude to transform even the worst of circumstances.

Tips for Practicing Gratitude

Before we begin practicing gratitude, I want to briefly share with you a few practical tips and guidelines for doing so. These are based both on research that's been conducted on gratitude, as well as my own clinical work with patients. Keep in mind that there are individual differences and no recommendation is "one size fits all." But when you begin your gratitude practice, you may want to keep these simple guidelines in mind:

Focus on the interpersonal: Studies show that focusing on *people* for whom or to whom you feel grateful has a greater effect on our well-being than focusing on more material *things* for which you feel grateful. This practice also serves the added purpose of helping to strengthen interpersonal bonds, which further helps to boost happiness.

Notice the small things: It's easy to gloss over seemingly banal or minor events in our everyday lives, but noticing and appreciating these small things can often be critical to the cultivation of gratitude in our lives.

Maintain a regular routine: Building any new habit takes time and effort to become part of your life, and we often stop doing things before we give them a chance to really work. Establishing a regular routine or ritual around gratitude can help us to integrate the practice into our lives in order to reap the benefits. Whether you set aside time each evening, over your lunch hour, or set gratitude "alarms" on your phone, I strongly encourage you to find ways to establish a rhythm of gratitude in your life.

Get some variety: In the next section you'll be learning about several evidence-based methods to incorporate the power of gratitude in your life. It's likely that one or two will resonate more for you, and that's great. Allow these to form the backbone of your gratitude work in the future. But be careful not to get stuck *only* using one or two methods, because studies show that variety is indeed the spice of life when it comes to gratitude. By varying our routines, we actually gain more benefit from our practice of gratitude.

Get Visual: Try putting up words or images of gratitude throughout your home, office, or even your car. These might be simple reminders, positive words of encouragement, or photos of people who you love. A personal favorite of mine is investing in a digital photo frame, where I store photos of some of my favorite people and memories in my life. This serves as a daily reminder, no matter what else is going on for me, of all that I have to be thankful for.

Don't just go through the motions: Just as it's important to incorporate variety into the *type* of gratitude exercises we practice, it's equally important to vary the *source* of gratitude we focus on. For example, one patient I worked with began writing in a gratitude journal, but each week he would identify the same five things he felt grateful for (namely his car, his dog, his health, his girlfriend, and his job). You can imagine how such a practice would have diminishing returns over time! Once he corrected this, he began to really reap the rewards of practicing gratitude. So be sure to challenge yourself to look closely and broadly in your life for things to be grateful for.

Be careful not to overdo it: Certain gratitude exercises you will be learning, such as "3 Good Things," are designed to be practiced daily for a period of time. But others, such as the "Gratitude Journal," have been shown to be susceptible to burnout effects. Some studies have shown, for example, that doing a gratitude journal on a weekly basis can actually be more potent that doing it three or more times per week. Similarly, periodically completing a "Gratitude Letter" every few months will be more powerful than if you were to do one each week, for example.

Don't worry about spelling, grammar, or punctuation: This one is fairly self-explanatory. But needless to say, the gratitude interventions discussed in this book are for *you*, so don't worry about what you write or how you write it.

Link up with a gratitude partner: Studies show that any new habit (whether a new diet, or a new exercise regimen) becomes much easier to follow when we have social support. By linking up with a friend or family member who can support you in this process, or even join in on the fun, it can become much easier to count your blessings and benefit from the practice of gratitude.

GRATITUDE PRACTICES

Gratitude Practice #1: Three Good Things

The first gratitude technique we'll be practicing is called "Three Good Things," which is adapted from Martin Seligman (2005). The instructions are pretty simple and the exercise won't take you long, but this can be one of the most powerful gratitude-boosting methods you'll encounter. I recommend buying a small notebook or journal in which to write, but feel free to do whatever is most comfortable for you. The most important thing is that you write down your "good things," and that you commit to this practice for at least two weeks, preferably longer.

Instructions: Each night for the next two weeks before you go to bed, please write down three things that went well for you that day. These good things can be relatively small or minor occurrences, or they can be larger and of greater significance to you. Below each positive event that you list, please write down an answer to the question "Why did this good thing happen?" or "What was my contribution to this good thing?" After two weeks, write a brief reflection on how this practice impacted your mood.

Example:

Good Thing #1: *I had a fulfilling day at work and my sessions with patients went well.*

Why this happened/My contribution: *I made sure I got plenty of sleep last night and tried to be very present and attuned in my sessions today.*

Good Thing #2: *My partner cooked my favorite dinner, spaghetti and meatballs.*

Why this happened/My contribution: *I expressed gratitude and thanked her the last time she cooked, and told her how much I appreciated it.*

Good Thing #3: *It was a beautiful and sunny day outside when I was driving to work.*

Why this happened/My Contribution: *I took the time to notice and appreciate the weather, instead of being on "autopilot" on my way to work.*

As you can see, the "good things" you come up with don't have to be earth shattering or groundbreaking. They can even be the small things that we often overlook, or are too busy to notice. Here, you try.

(Continued)

Practice:

Good Thing #1:

_____

_____

Why this happened/My contribution:

_____

_____

Good Thing #2:

_____

_____

Why this happened/My contribution:

_____

_____

Good Thing #3:

_____

_____

Why this happened/My Contribution:

_____

_____

A key point I want to emphasize is that it's important to focus on things that go well from *that day*, rather than things you feel *generally* grateful for in your life. We'll be getting to an exercise designed to tap into that type of gratitude later in this chapter, but for the purposes of this exercise you'll want to make sure you're identifying specific events that occurred, or that you noticed, that particular day. Also, if you want to take this exercise to the next level, and I strongly encourage you to, try making a rule for yourself that you *never repeat* an item over the exercise. For example, if you do this for two weeks, you'll end up coming up with forty two distinct "good things" to put in your journal!

As you continue to practice this technique, you'll notice a shift in your outlook and the way you view the world. Over time, you'll even find that you are seeking out things to be grateful for in anticipation of writing in your journal. This exercise also helps us to end our days on a positive note, which as we learned earlier in this chapter can help promote better sleep. So you'll not only feel happier and more grateful, you'll feel better rested too.

Gratitude Practice #2: The Gratitude Journal

Whereas the "Three Good Things" exercise highlights positive events that occur on a daily basis, the "Gratitude Journal" exercise is designed to bring more awareness to some of the more stable, overarching sources of gratitude in our lives. Gratitude expert Robert Emmons (2007) has demonstrated persuasively that doing this exercise can help significantly boost happiness, while also reducing stress and even improving our physical health. While the "Three Good Things" exercise is meant to be a daily practice, the "Gratitude Journal" may in fact be more effective as a weekly exercise.

Instructions: Our day-to-day lives are filled with both good and bad, but where we bring our focus and awareness is crucial. There are indeed always people and things in our lives that we might feel grateful for. Some of these may seem small, while others may be more profound. Reflect back over the past week, and in the space below please write five things for which you feel grateful or thankful. For the next 8 weeks, complete this exercise at least once per week. At the end of that time, reflect on how it has impacted your mood and your happiness.

Example:

Gratitude #1: I feel thankful for my health. Although I have been struggling with a back injury, I feel fortunate that my overall health is good and that I'm able to do most things that I'm passionate about.

Gratitude #2: I feel grateful for my partner. I feel particularly thankful that she has been so patient with me while I've been writing this book.

Gratitude #3: I feel thankful that my car works (knock on wood) because I can easily remember times in my life when money was tight and I'd cross my fingers each morning hoping it would start.

Gratitude #4: I feel grateful that I get to live in the Bay Area, one of the most beautiful places that I've ever experienced.

Gratitude #5: I am thankful for good colleagues, who I get to work side by side with each day doing valuable work while having fun.

As you can see, the sources of one's gratitude need not be profound, and can even include things that we might often gloss over or take for granted. Now that you get the idea, let's have you try.

(Continued)

Practice:

Gratitude #1:

_____

_____

Gratitude #2:

_____

_____

Gratitude #3:

_____

_____

Gratitude #4:

_____

_____

Gratitude #5:

_____

_____

Similarly to the "Three Good Things" exercise outlined above, the "Gratitude Journal" can profoundly shift our focus towards the more positive parts of our lives. As we've discussed at various points in this book, our minds tend to focus on the negative more readily than the positive and in fact, our brains were in some respects designed to focus on the negative from an evolutionary perspective. As a result, we need to find ways to counteract this tendency in order to boost our happiness and well-being. By creating and writing in a gratitude journal, we begin to do just that.

Troubleshooting Tip: Whereas some people seem to benefit from practicing this exercise daily, it has also been shown to be somewhat vulnerable to burnout effects. As we discussed earlier in this chapter, there is some evidence that weekly practice may in fact be superior to daily practice (Lyubomirsky, 2007). I recommend experimenting a bit to find your own personal preferences and optimal "dosing" for this exercise, but aim to start with one or two days per week and adjust accordingly from there.

Gratitude Practice #3: Our Inner George Bailey

Each year during the holiday season, you've probably flipped through the channels and seen *It's a Wonderful Life* on television. It turns out not only to be a great movie, but also offers valuable clues about the importance of gratitude, and how we might best practice it.

Without trying to give away too much, the film's protagonist (named George Bailey) becomes suicidal due to a financial setback, and decides to take his own life in order for his family to receive his life insurance settlement. He is rescued by a guardian angel named Clarence who proceeds to take George on a tour of what his world would look like if he had never been born. George witnesses his brother passing away prematurely, his children never being born, his beautiful wife struggling immensely, and his beloved hometown in shambles. So rather than ask George to reflect on what he was grateful for, Clarence had done something altogether different. **He had shown George a world in which those blessings had never come to pass, which demonstrated just how unique and special those gifts in fact were.**

Although most gratitude techniques work by helping us directly acknowledge our blessings, the tale of George Bailey offers us a different path altogether. But does this strategy actually work? And can we in fact learn from the lessons of *It's a Wonderful Life*? To test whether this tactic can indeed boost gratitude and happiness, a team of researchers decided to look at married couples (Koo et al., 2008). One group of subjects was simply asked to write a story about how they met their spouse. **But another group was instructed to write a story imagining what their life might look like if in fact they had never met their spouse. In other words, they were asked to tap into their inner "George Bailey." The results turned out to be quite remarkable.**

Although we might expect that the second exercise could perhaps be a bit depressing, the findings from this study suggested just the opposite. As it happened, the participants in the "George Bailey" condition who were asked to imagine *not* meeting their spouse ended up reporting significantly *higher* relationship satisfaction and feelings of happiness than those who merely re-told their story of falling in love. According to one of the main researchers in the study, psychologist Timothy Wilson, this may be due to the fact that this exercise helped make people's relationships seem, "surprising and special again, and maybe a little mysterious – the very conditions that prolong the pleasure we get from the good things in life." In other words, the "George Bailey" strategy may

(Continued)

help to counteract our tendency to adapt and habituate to even the best of things in our lives, as discussed earlier in Chapter 2 of this book.

So in addition to the more traditional gratitude-boosting strategies you begin practicing, I highly recommend incorporating the "George Bailey" technique from time to time as well. In a journal or on a separate piece of paper, use the following brief instructions to harness the power of this technique:

Instructions: Reflect for a moment on one particular person, opportunity, or experience in your life that brings you happiness or joy. Bask for a brief time in whatever feelings arise when you think about this. **In your journal, first write down all the various ways in which this person or experience might have not come into your life.** For example, if you met your spouse one day at a coffee shop, imagine all the ways in which that might not have occurred were it not due to fortuitous timing. **Once you've done so, reflect on what your life might look like today were it not for that person, opportunity, or experience.** Consider how different things would be, and how much would be missing, and write that down in your journal as well.

Although different from many of the gratitude techniques you're learning, the "George Bailey" technique has been shown to have powerful effects on our happiness and life satisfaction. By imagining the absence of something important to us, we are able to gain even greater appreciation for the joy we receive from it. Some people I've worked with have even described this as one of the most powerful gratitude-boosting strategies they've tried. I hope you find it similarly useful.

Gratitude Practice #4: Reflecting on Hardship

Many gratitude techniques are aimed at developing greater appreciation for our blessings. **But some studies show that a useful way to increase appreciation for our present circumstances can actually come from reflecting back on our struggles and times of hardship.** Robert Emmons calls this practice "remembering the bad." His findings suggest that by consciously thinking back to these difficult times in life, we actually create fertile ground for gratitude to spring forth (Emmons, 2007). I find that during periods of stress, this can be a particularly powerful strategy.

Instructions: Reflect back on a difficult time in your life, a time in which you struggled with pain, hardship, or heartache. Remember the feelings of sadness or even despair that you fought during your darkest hour. Try to be specific in recalling a particular memory or time period for this exercise. Notice the various thoughts, memories, images, and emotions that come to mind for you in this moment.

Now remember that no matter what occurred back then, you were able to overcome that suffering to be here today. Even the worst times of your life were merely temporary, and you had the strength to survive and live on. The fact that you are here today, able to remember these bad moments, is testimony to your strength and perseverance.

Many people report that by reflecting on these periods of hardship, they are able to gain a new perspective on their current situations. Challenges seem more surmountable, and obstacles can be viewed as temporary difficulties rather than permanent barriers. We often come to see that no matter how trying our current situation may be, it could always be worse. By contrasting our current circumstance with these negative times, we may even feel more grateful which can boost our happiness and well-being tremendously. **I strongly recommend using this exercise during periods of struggle**, in conjunction with the other gratitude exercises in this chapter.

Gratitude Practice #5: A Day of Thanks

As we discussed earlier, the practice of gratitude is often by nature an interpersonal endeavor. When we are grateful, we first recognize that our lives are filled with good fortune. Secondly, we acknowledge that the source of this goodness comes from outside of ourselves, which often includes others in our lives (Emmons, 2007). **In this exercise, you'll be working on not only acknowledging the good things that come your way, but also directly communicating your thanks to others who help make these good things possible.** Choose one day out of the month, and transform it into a day of expressing thanks.

__Instructions:__ Throughout our lives, we are often on the receiving end of kindness from others, ranging from those closest to us to even strangers. **Over the next month, choose one day to serve as your day of "thanks-giving."** On that day, go out of your way to express gratitude to everyone who treats you with kindness, even for seemingly small acts. Whether it's a person holding the door for you, or someone who asks you how your day went, go out of your way and verbally express your gratitude towards them. Notice how it feels to do this, and how people around you seem to respond. At the end of the day, write a brief reflection in your gratitude journal describing your experience.

Acknowledging all that we have to be grateful for is crucial to happiness. **But expressing gratitude to the people around us can bolster those feelings and strengthen our relationships.** Many individuals who engage in this particular gratitude practice find that doing so leads to a cascade of positivity in their relationships, whereby expressing thanks becomes a much more common and comfortable habit. Have fun with this one, and watch your relationships with others become even stronger as a result.

Bonus Gratitude Practice: Gratitude Letter and Visit

An immensely powerful gratitude exercise, the "Gratitude Letter and Visit" invites you to write a letter of thanks to someone important in your life, and to deliver the letter to that person. Although it's certainly a gratitude-based exercise, I've actually included it in Chapter 10 (The Path of Connection) of this book because of its interpersonal emphasis and its ability to foster closeness and connection. If you'd like to get a head start on this practice, feel free to jump ahead to that exercise at the end of Chapter 10, where you will find a more detailed description of the "Gratitude Letter and Visit" practice along with instructions on how to carry it out.

Chapter 5

The Path of Kindness and Altruism

"If you want to be happy, practice compassion"

—His Holiness, the Dalai Lama

THE POWER OF KINDNESS

An old story tells the tale of a rabbi who once experienced firsthand the difference between heaven and hell. Hell, so the story goes, consisted of a room in which a group of people sat around a large circular table. In the middle of the table rested a pot of stew, piping hot and plentiful. The stew smelled so delicious that it made the rabbi's mouth water in anticipation. And yet despite the bountiful amount of food on the table, which would have been more than sufficient to feed everyone there, nobody was eating.

As he looked closer, the rabbi noticed that each of the individuals sitting around the table possessed a long spoon as an eating utensil. Their arms had been splinted straight with wooden slats, such that they could not bend their elbows. Moreover, although the spoons were more than long enough to reach the pot of stew, they were too long to allow the people sitting around the table to feed themselves. And thus, despite the ample amount of food available to them, the people were starving. The rabbi felt heartbroken to see these poor souls and to hear their tortured groans, as they were so close to nourishment and yet unable to consume it.

After visiting this room, the rabbi asked to see heaven, and he was whisked away to a place similar to the one he had just visited. At first, the rabbi thought it looked identical to hell, and believed surely there had been some mistake. Much like the room where he had just visited, a group of people sat around a large table, with the very same stew resting in the center. He looked closer, and saw that indeed the people there had been supplied with the identical kind of long spoon as he had just seen, and that their arms were similarly splinted such that they could not bend their elbows. And yet despite these similarities, the people in this room appeared well-nourished, and there was much laughter in the air.

It was at this moment that the rabbi noticed one of the individuals sitting at the table reach his spoon into the stew, and feed the person sitting across the table from him. Sure enough, after taking a bite, that person returned the favor and fed his benefactor. The rabbi stood in wonderment as this very scene repeated itself into the night. Before long, all had received nourishment, and none were hungry. As he reflected on what he had witnessed, the rabbi came to believe that hell and heaven offered us the very same conditions and circumstances. The difference, he realized, was in how we choose to treat each other. Generosity and kindness, in this case, had the power to transform misery into joy, hunger into contentment, and hell into heaven.

****

We all know intuitively that practicing kindness and compassion towards those around us is a good thing. Whether through our families or our faith, many of us are taught from a young age that giving to others is a noble endeavor. The fact that practicing kindness is beneficial for those on the receiving end is self-evident. What may be less obvious, but no less important, are the immense benefits that practicing kindness can yield for the person who's doing the giving. In short, practicing kindness and compassion towards others has been shown to be one of the most effective ways of become happier and healthier.

This link between kindness and happiness is not exactly a novel concept. Indeed, religious scholars, philosophers, and other thinkers have proposed such a relationship for centuries. The famed British writer Henry James proposed that, "Three things in human life are important: the first is to be kind; the second is to be kind; and the third is to be kind." The poet William Wordsworth described the "little, nameless, unremembered acts of kindness and of love" as the "best portion of a good man's life." And the spiritual leader of Tibetan Buddhism, the Dalai Lama, promotes the idea that "If you want to be happy, practice compassion."

Recent research has shed light on the considerable benefits of practicing kindness and altruism. For the purposes of this chapter and for clarification, we will define kindness and altruism as acts in which we *do something for the benefit of another, with no direct measurable or material benefit to ourselves.* At times, this may come in the form of active giving, such as volunteer work, donating to charity, and so forth. However, giving may also come in the form of smaller or more private endeavors, such as offering emotional support to someone in need, or practicing small acts of kindness to others. Altruism and kindness will enable you to feel more connected to others around you, achieve a greater sense of meaning and purpose, and become a happier person.

KINDNESS: GOOD FOR OUR MINDS

We've all heard it been said that it's better to give than to receive. But recent findings in the field of mental health and happiness suggest that this old adage is more accurate than we could have ever imagined. Stephen Post, a professor of preventive medicine, and one of the world's foremost experts on kindness and compassion, describes giving to others as the "most powerful force on the planet." In his book, entitled *Why Good Things Happen to Good People*, Post outlines the various ways in which practicing kindness and altruism is beneficial for our mental health, physical health, and relationships.

Practicing kindness has been linked to benefits including increased happiness levels, a greater sense of meaning and purpose, and decreased rates of stress and mental illness (Schwartz, 2003). For example, a 2010 survey of individuals who regularly performed volunteer work found that ninety-two percent of those surveyed reported a greater sense of purpose and meaning in their lives, while eighty-nine percent expressed that volunteering had significantly boosted their overall well-being. Of course, correlation does not necessarily equate to causation, and these findings beg the question of "chicken versus egg" when it comes to the link between practicing kindness and happiness. Is it merely that happy people tend to be more generous and giving towards others? Or does the act of practicing kindness and giving actually *lead* to happiness?

Fortunately, happiness experts such as Sonja Lyubomirsky have attempted to shed light on this issue, with encouraging results. In one such study, she asked research participants to perform five acts of kindness one day per week for a period of six weeks. Both before and after the study, these individuals were assessed according to their happiness level, with the hopes of determining whether practicing kindness would actually directly increase their overall well-being. Impressively, it turned out that practicing kindness was strongly predictive of increases in happiness.

At the end of the six-week study, participants reported significant increases in overall happiness and well-being, far beyond their starting points at the outset of the research experiment (Lyubomirsky, 2007). For individuals coping with depression, it appears that giving behaviors are strongly linked to improvements in symptoms (Musick, 2003). Amazingly, this seems to hold true even among those individuals facing chronic and significant medical problems such as multiple sclerosis (Schwartz, 2003). Similarly, studies have shown that offering emotional support to those in need can reliably and effectively decrease anxiety even in times of high stress (Post, 2008). Practicing kindness and engaging in altruistic behaviors has further been shown to reduce stress levels, with one study showing that over seventy percent of people who volunteer report lower stress overall.

Even for individuals suffering from chemical dependency and addiction issues, the practice of kindness has been shown to yield immense benefits. One of the foremost experts in this area of research is psychologist Maria Pagano at Case Western University, who has shown through numerous studies that helping behavior and supporting others is strongly predictive of success in recovery for those individuals.

If you're a parent, you might also be interested to know that practicing kindness and engaging in altruism has been shown to have tremendous benefits to teenagers and adolescents. Among other things, teens who engage in generous behaviors are at reduced risk for depression and have significantly lower risk of suicide. They are also far less likely to fail subjects in school, become pregnant, and abuse alcohol or other substances. Moreover, they tend to display higher levels of self-esteem, and are more socially competent (Post, 2007). Amazingly, altruism during one's teenage years is strongly predictive of future happiness and well-being. In one study by Paul Wink, a psychologist at Wellesley College, prosocial and altruistic behaviors during high school was strongly connected to well-being even *fifty years* later!

In sum, practicing kindness and engaging in altruistic behaviors has been shown to promote happiness and boost our emotional well-being. Recent findings further demonstrate that giving to others results in even greater happiness than when we give to ourselves (Dunn and Norton, 2008). It turns out that the practice of kindness confers benefits even beyond the support we provide others and our own happiness. Namely, it has been shown to be one of the most powerful methods to strengthen our physical health, and even extend our lifespan.

KINDNESS: GOOD FOR OUR BODIES

You've probably seen the advertisements on television or in magazines for one of the many "wonder drugs" out there promising to lower cholesterol, eliminate depression, or reduce physical pain. Imagine seeing an ad for a new medication that could help give you more energy, decrease your aches and pains, reduce the impact of chronic illnesses, and even help to significantly increase your life expectancy and reduce mortality. If that drug ever came to the market, we'd probably all call our doctor immediately, or go running straight to the nearest pharmacy.

As it turns out, all of those benefits outlined above (and more) have been strongly connected to the practice of kindness. Stephen Post has spent years studying the health benefits of kindness and altruism. In his book, *Why Good Things Happen to Good People*, he summarizes many of the most exciting findings in this area, which are nothing shy of remarkable. In short, people who regularly practice kindness and altruism are not only happier; they're healthier too. Some studies even suggest that kindness and altruism has nearly as large of a benefit on health and longevity as quitting smoking!

One of the leading researchers in this area of study is Doug Oman of the University of California at Berkeley. A 1999 study by Oman and his colleagues examined the link between volunteer work and lifespan. Specifically, they looked at elderly individuals who volunteered regularly, and found that those who participated in two or more such activities had a *forty-four percent lower rate of mortality* than those who did not. This degree of benefit even exceeded that which people received from regular exercise (thirty percent), or being involved in religious activities (twenty-nine percent). The benefits of volunteering were found to hold true even after accounting for other possible explanations, such as marital status and overall physical health.

Another study by psychologist Stephanie Brown at the University of Michigan examined the impact of less structured, more day-to-day forms of giving. Examining elderly couples, Brown and her colleagues looked at the influence of helping behaviors on health and longevity. Examples of such behaviors included providing help to friends or neighbors, or offering emotional support to spouses during times of need. During the five-year period they assessed, Brown found that individuals who regularly engaged in helping behaviors and practiced kindness to others had a significantly reduced mortality rate compared to those who did less (Brown, 2003). A fascinating wrinkle from this study was that being on the receiving end of a person's kindness did not appear to hold nearly the same type of health or longevity benefits. So in order to live a long life, it certainly seems that it's better to give than to receive.

KINDNESS: GOOD FOR OUR LIVES

Scott Adams, the cartoonist best known for creating the *Dilbert* comic strip, once noted that there is "no such thing as a small act of kindness. Every act creates a ripple with no logical end." Reflect for a moment on a time in which you helped a person in need, or an instance in which someone came to your aid during a time of duress. Can you remember the feelings this generated for you, or the impact it had on your life? Chances are, the quote above rings true in your experience as well.

One of the powerful benefits of kindness comes with its ability to bring us closer to those around us, and foster our interpersonal connections. As Sonja Lyubomirsky explains, "Being kind and generous leads you to perceive others more positively and charitably." which "fosters a heightened sense of interdependence and cooperation in your social community" (Lyubomirsky, 2007). Although it's been said that, "nice guys finish last," exciting findings in the area of altruism suggest that the opposite is in fact true. Brent Simpson, a sociologist at the University of South Carolina, and an expert on social cooperation, has pointed out that when we give to others our kindness and generosity is often rewarded down the road leading to significant personal gains.

Some studies even suggest that our kind acts can create ripple effects up to three degrees outward. As James Fowler of UC San Diego explains, when one person behaves generously, this often inspires others to behave in the same way towards other individuals. As a result, "Each person in a network can influence dozens or even hundreds of people, some of whom he or she does not know and has not met" (Fowler and Christakis, 2010). Amazingly, the positive cascade that results from our acts of kindness can even help our bank accounts. Recent findings underscore the fact that practicing kindness to others can help reap financial benefits for the person doing the giving. This is likely a result of a sort of "pay it forward" phenomenon, in which recipients of our kind acts look to repay our generosity down the road.

Lastly, it should be noted that practicing kindness and compassion is good for our love lives. Those in romantic relationships know this to be true from experience, but scientific research backs up this assertion. In an investigation of 37 cultures around the world spanning over ten thousand individuals, psychologist David Buss sought to learn about which qualities were considered most desirable in a potential mate. After sifting through the data, Buss discovered that of all the potential qualities, ranging from physical attractiveness to income, the most important characteristic people identified was kindness (Buss, 1989). In fact, across all 37 cultures that were examined, kindness was the only quality that was considered universally desirable. So in love, as in life, it pays to practice kindness.

THIS IS YOUR BRAIN ON GIVING

Think about the last time you offered a helping hand to someone in need, whether it was through volunteer work or merely being there as a source of support during a difficult period. Do you remember what it felt like for you? You may recall feeling a sense of connection to that individual, a greater sense of meaning and purpose, and even a boost in self-esteem. But you might also remember feeling a bit of a "warm glow," or even a sense of euphoria. Believe it or not, there's a brain-based explanation for this feeling, and happiness researchers have come to call it the "helper's high."

Allan Luks coined this term, and he described the phenomenon of the "helper's high" in his book, *The Healing Power of Doing Good* (Luks, 2001). By studying over three thousand volunteers, Luks demonstrated the various positive benefits that come from doing volunteer work, ranging from better health outcomes to increased happiness. But one of the most mind-blowing findings was the idea that our brain responds in unique ways to the act of giving, resulting in a feeling of euphoria when we practice kindness. In short, giving to others can lead us to feel an intense rush, or even a "high."

Recent imaging studies of the brain provide clues as to why people often experience these intense positive feelings when they give to others. In a 2006 study, neuroscientist Jorge Moll and his colleagues at the National Institute of Health attempted to examine what happens in our brains when we engage in charitable giving. Amazingly, Moll discovered that charitable giving resulted in an activation of the pleasure centers in our brains, which perhaps accounts for the "warm glow" feeling often reported by those who perform acts of kindness.

Scientists also suspect that engaging in altruistic behaviors results in a release of endorphins in our brain, which would explain the rush we often feel when we engage in giving behaviors. Stephen Post has even suggested that in these instances our brain likely releases more of the neurotransmitter dopamine, which is linked to pleasure and reward in our brains. Finally, studies have shown that when we give to others, the very same areas of our brains become activated as when we receive a financial gift. Perhaps giving truly is better than receiving, after all.

How and Why Does Kindness Work?

It might seem surprising at first that this relatively straightforward practice can lead to such profound benefits across so many areas. However, a closer look at the mechanisms by which kindness works helps shed some light on its power.

First, as described in the previous section, engaging in kind acts helps to literally change our brain. Our pleasure and reward centers become activated, and there is a likely release of both dopamine and endorphins, which helps account for the "high" we often experience when we help others. A second explanation for the power of kindness stems from the tendency for our good deeds to be rewarded by others whom we help down the road. In other words, people tend to repay our kindness during our own times of need, resulting in both material and emotional benefits, a process referred to as "reciprocal altruism" (Trivers, 1971).

A third basis for the impact of kindness and altruism has to do with its impact on our own self-esteem and sense of meaning. Reflect for a moment on a time when you provided emotional or practical support for another person. Chances are, you not only felt glad to help that individual, but it made you feel good about yourself too. When we give to others, we become more aware of our own positive qualities and can appreciate our generosity and compassion. This leads us to experience a greater sense of meaning and purpose, along with improved feelings of self-worth.

Fourth, practicing kindness towards others enables us to view our own struggles in a different light. We all fall prone to the occasional tendency to become consumed by day-to-day stressors, the importance of which we often magnify. This tendency to "not see the forest for the trees" can be directly counteracted through practicing kindness and compassion to others. When we engage in such practices, we become better equipped to step out of ourselves and gain a new perspective on our difficulties. We may even find ourselves able to feel more grateful for the blessings we do have in our lives. As the psychologist Viktor Frankl once noted, "The more one forgets himself – by giving himself to a cause to serve or another person to love – the more human he is and the more he actualizes himself."

Finally, kindness and altruism possess such great power to transform our lives because they help foster and nurture our interpersonal relationships. As discussed at various points in this book, social connection is one of our greatest emotional protective factors, and the absence of social support is strongly correlated with ailments such as depression and low self-esteem. This is particularly problematic in our current day and age, in which individuals work longer hours at their jobs and are often socially isolated. Indeed, as the political scientist Robert Putnam has pointed out, more and more Americans find themselves "bowling alone" in an increasingly disconnected society (Putnam, 2000). Through practicing kindness and altruism, we become reconnected to the world around us and cultivate our interpersonal relationships. We protect ourselves against stress and depression, obtain support from those around us, and achieve a greater sense of purpose and connection in our lives.

GIVING WHEN TIMES ARE TOUGH

During times of good fortune and comfort, it can often feel easier to be giving and practice kindness to others. And yet, there may be no better time to practice compassion than in periods of struggle and adversity. Earlier in this chapter, we discussed the benefits of practicing kindness on our health. There is now considerable evidence pointing to the importance of doing so even when our physical or emotional health is suffering. In fact, practicing kindness and altruism has been shown to have uniquely beneficial effects even for those struggling with chronic or even terminal illnesses.

Stephen Post has persuasively demonstrated that for individuals suffering from conditions ranging from multiple sclerosis (MS) to HIV/AIDS, the act of reaching out to others who shared their struggle was strongly connected to better psychological outcomes. For example, one study of women suffering with MS revealed that those who volunteered for others experienced gains in terms of psychological adjustment *seven times* higher than those who had received help (Lyubomirsky, 2007). Keep in mind that the forms of helping that we're talking about need not be groundbreaking or time-consuming. Examples included running small errands, driving individuals to medical appointments, or doing small bits of housework. And yet even these small acts of kindness appeared to have huge implications in terms of health and emotional adjustment.

By giving to others, particularly those who share our own struggles, we can transcend our current plight and transform our lives. When I reflect on this, I always think back to a patient I used to work with whom we will call Jermaine. I met Jermaine during my predoctoral internship at a Veterans Affairs hospital, and he had recently returned from a tour of duty in Afghanistan. Like many young men returning from war, Jermaine had mixed emotions that he was grappling with. On the one hand he felt pride about his service to his country, and immense loyalty towards those he had fought with. And yet Jermaine had experienced significant trauma while in combat overseas, which had shaken him to the core. When I first began working with him, Jermaine had been experiencing significant symptoms of posttraumatic stress disorder, including terrifying nightmares, crippling anxiety, and an inability to work or function well in his life and relationships.

Progress was slow, and despite participating in both group and individual therapy, as well as receiving psychiatric medications, Jermaine continued to struggle. It was a few months into our work together that Jermaine experienced a major turning point. He arrived excitedly to one of our sessions, and explained that earlier in the week an older veteran had befriended him after a support group and taken Jermaine under his wing. According to Jermaine, this other individual had fought in the Vietnam War, and for years had suffered through anger, guilt, and bitterness. After undergoing successful treatment for PTSD, this older veteran had decided to reach out to younger vets returning home, in the hopes that they would not have to repeat the same sort of pain and anguish that he had gone through. Jermaine became tearful when describing how this act had affected him, and had opened his eyes to the possibility of a better future. "I know I've got a long road ahead of me," he told me, "but I know there's hope and that I'm not alone."

Over time, Jermaine became so touched and inspired by the kindness he had received that he decided to repay others in the same way. As he continued to progress in his own recovery, he began befriending and mentoring other young veterans returning home from war. As he explained to me, "When I meet these young kids coming home, I know that I gotta keep doing the right thing for me but also for them now." When I left the hospital at the end of my training year, Jermaine was like a different person. He had returned to the work force, and had become a peer counselor for other veterans returning home from combat. The kindness that Jermaine received had helped him heal, which in turn inspired him to want to do the same.

TIPS FOR PRACTICING KINDNESS

Just as in our chapter on gratitude, I'd like to first briefly share a few practical tips and guidelines for practicing kindness and compassion.

> ***Consider "bunching up" your kind acts:*** Some research, including work done by Sonja Lyubomirsky (2007), suggests that it's better to cluster rather than space out our acts of kindness. For example, one study found that participants who completed five acts of kindness on a single day, rather than five over the course of a week, reaped greater rewards in terms of happiness. This may be due to

the fact that a single act of kindness may not stand out above our norm, whereas completing multiple acts within the course of the day might provide a larger boost. I recommend experimenting a bit to find your own optimal "dosage."

Get Personal: When we practice kindness towards others directly, we receive an even greater boost in happiness. So when you can, try to perform acts of kindness that bring you face to face with other individuals. This will help you experience more of that "warm glow" or "helper's high" we described earlier in this chapter.

Get some variety: Think back to Chapter 2, when you learned about the notion of hedonic adaptation, which can act as a sort of kryptonite for happiness. One of the key ways to avoid burnout or adaptation in our happiness work is to vary things up and avoid over-repetition. I recommend varying both *how* and *when* you perform acts of kindness. Try rotating things around a bit in order to achieve better results.

Push your comfort zone: In order to receive the full benefits of practicing kindness, try not to merely repeat something you're already doing. Rather, I encourage you to push beyond your comfort zone and seek out new ways to practice kindness. For example, if you already spend some time each week tutoring your younger brother in math, that's excellent and you will already have gotten a head start. But try and discover additional ways to engage in altruism to truly reap the full rewards.

Don't worry about size or scale: Some patients I've worked with have gotten tripped up over aiming too high when it comes to performing acts of kindness. Small gestures, such as stopping and talking to a homeless person on the street, giving up your seat on the subway for an elderly person, or volunteering an hour of your time to a community organization, are more than sufficient. As historian Howard Zinn once reflected, "Small acts, when multiplied by millions of people, can transform the world."

Find a cause you believe in: When we participate in activities that give us a sense of meaning or purpose, we become more connected to them emotionally and are more likely to repeat them. So consider particular causes for which you have a passion, whether it be combatting homelessness, improving our education system, fighting poverty, or helping to keep our environment clean.

Whatever matters most to you can serve as a compass of sorts for your acts of kindness. By combining altruism with a deeper sense of meaning, you'll reap even greater benefits in terms of happiness.

Be mindful of resentments: Every once in a while our practice of kindness can backfire, and even lead to feelings of anger or resentment. One of the ways this can happen is if you find yourself performing kind acts out of obligation or guilt, or if it's done to the point of feeling overwhelmed. For example, some research on caregivers of individuals suffering from chronic illness suggests that their health and minds suffer due to the inherent stress they experience from helping. This can lead to unpleasant feelings festering, and can actually have a strongly negative impact on emotional and physical health. So be mindful of any anger or resentment that arises, and be sure to take care of yourself if you begin to feel overwhelmed at any point.

Have fun with it. Any habit becomes easier to maintain when it feels fun and rewarding. So whether it's through finding ways to give that are pleasurable, or by linking up with a "kindness partner" to help keep you motivated, it helps to make the practice of kindness even more fun and enjoyable.

Kindness Practices

Kindness Practice #1: Five Acts of Kindness

The first kindness exercise we'll be practicing invites you to engage in small acts of kindness towards others. It's an exercise adapted from one created by happiness researcher Sonja Lyubomirsky (2007), and has been strongly connected with increases in happiness. For the purposes of this practice, it's important to remember that there's nothing too big or too small, and there are no right or wrong answers. The possibilities are endless, so don't get too caught up in overthinking it.

Instructions: In our everyday lives, we all perform acts of kindness towards others, and receive similar kindness as well. Some of these acts may be small, while others may seem much larger in scope. Sometimes the person for whom the kind act is being performed may not even be aware of the act. Examples of kind acts include donating blood, volunteering at a community agency, helping paint a friend's house, feeding a stranger's expired parking meter or bringing coffee to work for a colleague. **Over the next week, choose a single day of the week to serve as your "kindness day," and perform five acts of kindness towards others on that day.** Repeat this practice for at least four weeks.

Over the month (or more) that you engage in this practice on a weekly basis, I recommend keeping a small journal to keep track of the kind acts you perform, as well as the emotional impact they have on you. This serves two purposes: first, it maintains personal accountability to help you keep track of your kind acts; second, you'll learn about how engaging in these acts affects you on a personal level, providing you with a sense of which ones you'd like to keep building on in the future.

Example:

Kindness Day/Date: Tuesday, November 11

Kind Act #1: This morning, I brought coffee for the support staff at work.

Kind Act #2: Today, I sent a small donation for disaster relief efforts in the Philippines following a recent storm.

Kind Act #3: This afternoon, I smiled and asked the grocery store checkout clerk how her day was going.

Kind Act #4: This evening, I sent a message checking in on a friend I haven't seen in a few years.

(Continued)

Kind Act #5: Today, I tracked down and personally thanked a co-worker for their excellent and hard work with a mutual patient.

Impressions: Performing a few of these small acts of kindness not only felt good, it turned out to be fun, too. I especially enjoyed doing things that brought me face to face with other people, so that I could directly see the impact of my kindness on them. For example, when I brought coffee in for our support staff I could really see how touched and appreciative they were. I think in the future I'd like to keep coming up with ways to directly interact with others during my kind acts, because that seems to feel especially meaningful to me.

When you practice this in the coming week, feel free to use the following template to keep track of your progress:

Practice:

Kindness Day/Date: _____

Kind Act #1: _____

Kind Act #2: _____

Kind Act #3: _____

Kind Act #4: _____

Kind Act #5: _____
Impressions: _____

How this exercise works: As the findings in this chapter have shown, practicing kindness can have a profound impact on our happiness as well as our health. When we perform even small acts of kindness, we feel more connected to those around us, experience a greater sense of purpose and meaning, and often feel a boost in self-esteem. Moreover, we are able to gain a new perspective on our own lives, and feel a measure of gratitude for the good things we experience.

Troubleshooting Tips: While some people have proposed doing one small act of kindness each day, research has shown that it may be better to "bunch up" our kind acts rather than space them out. I would recommend trying to perform all five acts of kindness on a single day per week, and adjusting from there accordingly based on your own fit. I also encourage you to be creative in the ways in which you give, as variety can help prevent this activity from becoming stale.

Kindness Practice #2: Better to Give Than to Receive?

Earlier in this chapter, you learned about the many benefits of practicing kindness. In my opinion, one of the most exciting findings has been the discovery that it may truly be better to give than to receive, both from an emotional and physical health standpoint. **Indeed, in terms of happiness and health, it appears that the benefit of giving to others exceeds the benefit of receiving.** In this next exercise, you'll be putting this theory to the test in your own life as you compare and contrast what it's like to give versus receive. This exercise has been adapted from Martin Seligman (2006) and Chris Peterson (2006), and has been shown to have powerful effects in terms of boosting our happiness.

Instructions: Over the next week, please choose one activity to engage in that's purely for fun or personal pleasure, and one that's for the benefit of another individual. Be sure that the two activities you choose are roughly comparable in terms of time and effort (for example, we wouldn't compare going to a three-hour concert with holding the door for someone). At the end of the week, once you've completed the two activities, please respond to the following questions. Feel free to use a separate piece of paper for more space.

- What activity did you engage in for yourself?
- What did you do for someone else?
- How did it feel doing the pleasurable activity? What emotions were most prominent?
- How did it feel doing the activity for someone else? What emotions did you notice?
- What differences did you notice in terms of how these activities made you feel?
- Did either activity seem to have a longer or more potent effect?
- Did you learn anything, or notice anything surprising through this experience?

Most people who complete this exercise observe that both activities yield positive emotions but with some important differences. Whereas the purely pleasurable activity often results in fleeting feelings of happiness, the altruistic activity tends to lead to deeper feelings of

(Continued)

connection, meaning, and well-being. Test it out this week, and see how it goes for you.

Troubleshooting Tip: As mentioned in the instructions, try to ensure that the two activities are roughly equivalent in terms of time and effort, which will allow a more equal comparison.

Kindness Practice #3: Volunteering for a Cause

We've discussed throughout this chapter some of the amazing benefits that have been shown to result from engaging in volunteer work. **These include lower levels of stress, increased happiness and life satisfaction, a deeper sense of meaning and purpose, and even a longer life!** Our next kindness exercise invites you to engage in the practice of volunteer work. It's important to remember that it doesn't take a tremendous time commitment in order to reap the emotional and physical benefits of volunteering. Even committing to doing an hour or two every few months is often sufficient to boost happiness levels that contribute to a deeper sense of meaning and purpose. Of course if you end up feeling inspired to do more, that's OK too.

To help you determine the best path to take in terms of determining volunteer opportunities, I recommend brainstorming a few different topics:

- *Passions:* What types of causes, issues, and subjects seem to stoke your passions and rouse your interests?
- *Skills:* What types of skills or abilities do you possess that may be of service to others?
- *Needs:* What sort of demand exists for the issues that you're passionate about?
- *Scale and scope:* Do you want to be involved in a larger cause, perhaps a worldwide issue such as environmentalism or international aid? Or do you prefer to feel connected to your immediate community?
- *Time:* How much time do you feel able to give? Do you want to do something that's ongoing, or would you prefer to find a one-time opportunity to start?

Once you've brainstormed, begin exploring possible opportunities you can become involved in. There are some great websites such as volunteermatch.com and serve.gov that can help point you in the right direction once you've narrowed your interests down a bit. **After you do engage in some direct volunteer work, I highly recommend writing a small journal entry about your experiences.** Reflect on what it was like for you, how it felt to give in this way, and how you might like to build on this experience in the future.

Kindness Practice #4: Recalling Kindness

While many studies demonstrate the immense benefits of engaging in new acts of kindness, other findings (Ortake, 2006) suggest that it may be equally important to step back and acknowledge the ways in which we already give. **In other words, rather than focusing solely on expanding our kindness practice, it is just as crucial that we acknowledge and appreciate the ways we already practice altruism.** This next exercise, which is designed to be practiced on a weekly basis, helps you do just that.

Instructions: In our lives, we all practice acts of kindness and compassion to those around us. Oftentimes, we do so without much conscious awareness, as it may come easily to us or occur without a second thought. Recent findings in the field of happiness suggest that it may be quite beneficial to step back, notice, and savor the ways in which we help others in our lives. Looking back over the past week, think about the ways in which you have helped others in your day-to-day life. These acts of kindness may be seemingly small, such as offering a friendly smile to a stranger. Or they may be more significant, such as mowing the lawn for an elderly couple down the street, or volunteering at a local soup kitchen. No matter the size or scope, reflect on the ways in which you have practiced kindness over the past week, and write down five such examples. Repeat this exercise on a weekly basis for at least one month.

For example, a patient of mine whom we'll call Christine began practicing this technique on a weekly basis. On the first week, her journal entry went as follows:

Kind Act #1: *Called a friend who was fighting with her husband to check in on her.*

Kind Act #2: *Gave $2 to the person in front of me on line at the supermarket, because he was short on money.*

Kind Act #3: *Put money in a stranger's parking meter which had just expired.*

Kind Act #4: *Smiled and said hello to the security guard at work.*

Kind Act #5: *Sent a birthday card to my grandmother.*

Now that you've seen her example, reflect back over the past week and think about how you might complete this exercise. Remember, the kind acts you engage in need not be large. Here, you try.

(Continued)

Kind Act #1: _____

Kind Act #2: _____

Kind Act #3: _____

Kind Act #4: _____

Kind Act #5: _____

Almost immediately, Christine noticed that she began feeling better as a result of engaging in this practice. "I haven't been doing anything different," she told me one day, "but I'm learning that I do more than I realized." Christine began feeling a greater sense of self-worth and self-esteem, and the more she noticed her kindness and the impact it had on others, the more she felt inspired to do even more. I hope and expect that it will have similar results for you.

Kindness Practice #5: The Gift of Time

We live in a fast-paced world, one that seems to be growing faster with each passing day. From the food we eat, to the way we communicate with each other, our world continues to trend in the direction of brevity and efficiency. Although there are benefits to this development, there are undoubtedly costs as well. Whereas close, face-to-face connection used to be the norm in previous generations, today our interpersonal relations often consist primarily of text messages, emails, and "tweets." This lack of true connection can lead to feelings of alienation and isolation, and may be directly tied to the rising rates of mental illness that we discussed in Chapter 2 of this book. Just as the "slow food" movement has caught fire as an antidote to our fast food culture, we must also work consciously to reestablish our close interpersonal connections to one another. This next Kindness exercise invites you to do just that.

Instructions: For this act of kindness, reflect on someone in your life who may be going through a time of difficulty or hardship. Perhaps this is a friend, a parent or grandparent, or a co-worker. If geographically possible, schedule a time in the near future to spend time with this individual face-to-face to offer some much needed support. If unable to do so, arrange to speak with them over the phone. Block out a sizable chunk of your day, turn off your cell phone, and try to be as present for the person as you can. Afterwards, reflect on what the experience was like for you, and how this act of kindness seemed to impact the other individual.

Most people who complete this exercise find that its personal touch brings about substantial feelings of warmth and connection, and can help strengthen their interpersonal relationships. I look forward to its doing the same for you.

Chapter 6

The Path of the Present Moment

"We're so busy watching out for what's just ahead of us that we don't take time to enjoy where we are."

—Bill Watterson

LIVING IN THE MOMENT

Several years ago, I had the good fortune of visiting Africa and going on a safari. As a lifelong animal lover, this was truly a dream come true for me. Being able to see lions, giraffes, and elephants in their natural habitat was incredibly thrilling and something I will never forget. What I didn't anticipate, however, was that I was also about to learn an important lesson about the power of the mind.

It was mid-morning, and our group was in the Serengeti Preserve in Tanzania. The weather was perfect, sunny but not too hot, and the morning had already been action-packed in terms of spotting animals. I was glancing down at my camera, hastily editing a few of the pictures I had taken and changing the setting, when out of the corner of my eye I saw something dart across the plain. When I looked up, I saw a lioness in hot pursuit of an impala. The lion sprinted after its prey, closing in with fierce tenacity. The impala, sensing imminent danger, looked up from grazing on the grass and bolted as fast as it could. The lion closed in, and the impala was almost within its reach. At the last instant, the impala turned and was able to gain some separation from its pursuer. The lion slowed down slightly and then stopped, unable to continue its chase. Its meal would have to come later.

Our jeep rolled towards where the impala was now standing, a hundred yards or so away. My heart was racing, and I could feel the adrenaline coursing through my veins. Sweat began to drip off my forehead, and I had to make a conscious effort to steady my hands. As we pulled up alongside the animal,

75

it would have been hard to imagine that such a frightening scenario had unfolded just moments before. The impala didn't appear alarmed; rather, she had resumed grazing on the tall grass. She appeared completely at ease again, with no indication that her life had nearly come to an unfortunate end just earlier.

As I looked on, continuing to breathe heavily while gripping the handle on the inside of our jeep, I felt someone pat me softly on the shoulder. Our guide, Winston, must have sensed my unease and was now looking at me with a slight grin. "You're more shaken up than she is," he exclaimed, gently poking fun at my fright. He motioned over to the impala, which continued to eat the grass with seemingly not a care in the world. "Once the chase is over," he said, "the hunter goes back to sleep, and the hunted goes back to eating. They don't think about it, they just do what they do." He continued, "If that happened to us, we'd be thinking about it for hours, days, even years. But the impala is different. The impala just lives in the moment. That's why she's so peaceful."

****

Do you find it hard to slow down and merely be present? Does your mind tend to wander back towards the past, or constantly glance forward towards the future? For many of us, it's all too easy to fall into this pattern of feeling stuck on "autopilot," mindlessly rushing through things without much conscious awareness, and focusing incessantly on the finish line with little connection to the process.

This state of *mindlessness* is incredibly common, particularly in our frenzied and often chaotic modern world. Unlike the impala from earlier in the chapter, we have a difficult time simply "grazing" in our everyday lives. Rather, many of us find ourselves constantly flooded with worry, regret, and fear. In his fascinating and fun book, *Why Zebras Don't Get Ulcers,* Stanford biologist Robert Sapolsky describes this very phenomenon and contrasts it with what occurs in the animal kingdom. As he explains, stress for animals tends to be episodic, while for humans it is often chronic. As a result, stress-related problems such as ulcers and hypertension are far less common among animals in the wild as compared to humans.

Like the impala on the Serengeti, animals quickly return to their natural baseline once a threat passes. They don't ruminate or stew over the danger they averted, they simply return to grazing. As Sapolsky humorously asks, "how many hippos worry about whether social security is going to last as long as they will, or what they are going to say on a first date?" We humans, however, are not so fortunate. We are constantly anticipating dangers that lie ahead, or lamenting losses from the past. This perpetual state of arousal raises our stress levels, which in turn can lead to a host of other problems including depression, anxiety, and physical health risks.

Our tendency toward mindlessness may feel deeply ingrained, yet in fact it's quite changeable. But how can we break this harmful habit of the mind? As it turns out, the answer may lie in an ancient practice, one that modern science and psychology is only recently starting to catch up to. The practice is called *mindfulness*, and it has been shown to have powerful, even life-changing effects on our mental health, physical health, and happiness.

Through the practice of mindfulness, we are able to become more fully immersed in the present moment, and break the chain of stress and worry. The goal isn't to necessarily become the impala from earlier, blissfully in the moment at all times. That would be neither practical nor realistic in our modern world. But we can certainly learn to take a page from her, in order to slow down our frenzied and often chaotic lives. We can all benefit from becoming more at one with the present moment, for reasons that will be explored more fully in this chapter. Mindfulness shows us how.

WHAT IS MINDFULNESS?

Reflect for a moment on the last time you found yourself stuck on "autopilot," or preoccupied in thought. It's all too common in our everyday lives to find ourselves aimlessly shifting from task to task, with little conscious awareness of where we are, or what we're doing. Conversely, think about the last time you found your mind wandering, perhaps thinking about the past or the future, with little connection to your surroundings. Common examples of these types of experiences in our everyday lives include:

- Driving to or from work, with little memory of the actual experience
- Eating a meal or snack despite not being hungry
- Ruminating many hours later about something your boss said to you at work
- Daydreaming

These sorts of experiences are quite common, and may seem harmless enough on the surface. But over time they can actually wreak havoc on our mental health and emotional well-being. We can fall into self-destructive patterns without realizing it, and have little conscious awareness of what we're doing and why. We become disconnected from life, missing out on what's happening right in front of our eyes. Researchers have even found that there is a direct cost to a wandering mind. Indeed, one well-known study even showed that our mind is wandering nearly as often as it is actually focused on what's in front of us. Worse yet, we tend to be least happy in those moments when our mind is wandering (Killingsworth & Gilbert, 2010).

The antidote to this state of mindlessness is in fact *mindfulness*. Mindfulness is an ancient practice, one that's been around for thousands of years but has only recently become understood and appreciated from a scientific perspective. Though definitions vary, mindfulness generally refers to maintaining moment-to-moment awareness of our thoughts, bodily sensations, feelings, and surrounding environment. Moreover, mindfulness involves acceptance and non-judgment, meaning that we observe and experience what's happening around and within us, without wishing for things to be any different than they are.

One of the world's foremost experts on mindfulness, Jon Kabat-Zinn, has summarized the experience of mindfulness as "paying attention in a particular way; on purpose, in the present moment, and nonjudgmentally" (Kabat-Zinn, 2013). Meditation instructor Guy Armstrong has likewise referred to mindfulness as "knowing what you are experiencing, while you are experiencing it." When we are mindful, we tune in to our experience in the present moment, rather than anxiously anticipating the future or regretfully pouring over the past. We become immersed in what's happening in the moment, without criticism or judgment.

Though mindfulness is often equated with meditation, it's actually a much broader concept. Rather than be viewed as a narrow technique, it is perhaps more fruitful to think of mindfulness as a different way of viewing the world. At its core, mindfulness helps us spend more time in the present moment, and can be seen as a form of mental training (Williams & Penman, 2011). Though it can be described in words, mindfulness is an experience that cannot be conveyed *only* in words. Rather, it requires practice and participation to fully experience it and reap its benefits. So after we describe some of the exciting and key findings when it comes to mindfulness, we'll be practicing some techniques to help you get started. But first, let's first dispel some myths about mindfulness, and talk about how to overcome some common obstacles in our path.

BARRIERS TO MINDFULNESS

In some respects, the practice of mindfulness is all the rage these days. In magazines and on bookshelves, on television and on the web, it seems like mindfulness is everywhere we look. Yet despite its growing popularity, there are nonetheless many misconceptions about the nature of mindfulness, some of which act as barriers to people adopting this valuable practice. In my clinical practice, I've often found that in addition to helping to teach what mindfulness is, it's just as important to explain what mindfulness is *not*. So with that in mind, here are some common examples of what mindfulness is not:

- *Mindfulness is not just meditation.* Mindfulness is actually a much broader concept than merely meditation, which can in turn take many different forms as well, beyond mindfulness. Instead, mindfulness can best be viewed as increasing our attention and awareness in the present moment.

- *Mindfulness is not wiping your mind clear of thoughts.* On the contrary, mindfulness is about becoming aware of your thoughts, but without judgment or attempting to push them away. Our brains will always produce thoughts – that's a fact of life. Rather than trying to suppress our thoughts, mindfulness shows us a path towards developing a more symphonic relationship with our thoughts and feelings.

- *Mindfulness is not relaxation.* You may at times feel relaxed as a byproduct of your mindfulness practice, and over time it can certainly help us become more relaxed and calm. But the overarching practice of mindfulness is not aimed at becoming more relaxed.

- *Mindfulness is not religion.* Though it owes some of its heritage to Buddhist philosophy, mindfulness can also be practiced in a wholly secular manner and requires no religious affiliation whatsoever.

- *Mindfulness is not sitting in a lotus posture and burning incense.* Needless to say, you certainly can do this if you'd like to, but it's far from a requirement of mindfulness!

Beyond these barriers and misconceptions outlined above, it should also be noted that much of our modern world makes the practice of mindfulness inherently more difficult. We are constantly inundated by distractions, and encouraged to multitask incessantly. Learning to slow down, or to become immersed the present moment, isn't exactly encouraged most of the time.

Given these roadblocks, many people find themselves frustrated and discouraged when they begin practicing mindfulness. "I can't slow down my thoughts," and "my mind is going every which way" are common experiences many of my patients encounter when they are just starting out. Fortunately, with patience and practice mindfulness becomes much easier and more natural over time. Furthermore, the very act of noticing one's wandering mind and consciously redirecting it to the present moment has been shown to be one of the most beneficial components of mindfulness. So even if you're a naturally distractible person, or find that your mind wanders a great deal, worry not. Simply noticing these tendencies and gradually retraining your mind to become more present-focused can in fact be hugely beneficial.

MINDFULNESS: GOOD FOR OUR MINDS

Although each path to happiness outlined in this book is backed by a great deal of scientific research, the findings related to mindfulness are particularly impressive. There have now been literally hundreds of studies done on the various benefits of practicing mindfulness, with seemingly more hitting the press each day. And the bottom line of these various studies is that mindfulness has the potential to improve our mental and emotional health in ways that are nothing short of incredible.

On the whole, individuals who regularly practice mindfulness perform better on a host of mental health outcomes, including an increased presence of positive emotions, coupled with lower rates of stress and anxiety (Keng, 2011). They furthermore appear to be happier and more content on average than their less mindful counterparts, a finding that has been replicated across a number of studies over the years (Ivanowski, 2007; Shapiro et al., 2008).

Those who practice mindfulness tend to be more optimistic as well, and report higher levels of overall life satisfaction (Lyubomirsky, 2008). Practicing mindfulness has even been shown to improve our attention and focus (Moore, 2012), and may even enhance memory. When stressors hit (as they do for all of us), individuals who regularly utilize mindfulness have been shown to engage in healthier and more effective coping strategies than their less mindful peers, suggesting that mindfulness enhances problem-solving enables us to make better choices (Weinstein, 2009).

Though the above findings are indeed remarkable, the connection between mindfulness and depression is particularly exciting. As it turns out, practicing mindfulness has been shown to dramatically decrease the likelihood of developing depression, and has even been demonstrated as a potent form of treatment among those who suffer from illnesses such as major depression. Mindfulness-based approaches have now been shown to be remarkably effective in the treatment of depression, on par with many traditional methods of psychotherapy and medication treatment (Williams and Penman, 2011). The effectiveness of mindfulness as a form of relapse prevention for depression is perhaps most promising. In one well-known study, researchers compared mindfulness training to ongoing medication management among individuals who had previously struggled with depression. They found that eight weeks of mindfulness training yielded the same preventive effects as antidepressants, and obviously without any unwanted side effects.

MINDFULNESS: GOOD FOR OUR BODIES

As exciting as the above findings certainly are, the impact of mindfulness on our physical health and well-being is perhaps equally impressive. There have now been a number of studies examining the effect of mindfulness on things like our overall physical health, sleep habits, and response to illnesses. As you probably surmised, mindfulness has been shown to have a powerful positive impact across these and other domains. In short, mindfulness not only feels good; it's good *for* us.

Individuals who practice mindfulness have been shown to have better overall physical health, require fewer doctors' visits, and spend fewer days in the hospital than their less mindful peers (Williams and Penman, 2011). You may of course be wondering whether it's simply a matter that healthier people may tend to be more mindful, rather than the other way around. Amazingly, it appears that mindfulness can in fact *cause* us to become healthier!

In one distinguished study, researchers compared newly trained mindfulness meditators to individuals who had received no training at all in mindfulness. After just eight weeks, they found that mindfulness training resulted in better immune system functioning, and that the meditators had generated more antibodies in response to the flu vaccine as compared to the non-meditators (Davidson & Kabat-Zinn, 2003). A later study found that among HIV-positive patients, mindfulness training was strongly connected to having a higher number of CD4$^+$ T cells in the body. These cells play a crucial role in our immune system functioning, and help protect us against attack. Amazingly, it appeared that the more people practiced mindfulness, the higher their CD4$^+$ T cell count was at the end of the study (Creswell, 2009).

If you suffer from chronic pain, as so many people do these days, it turns out that mindfulness can help you there, too. In a well-known study on the impact of mindfulness-based stress reduction (MBSR) on chronic pain, researchers found that mindfulness practice dramatically decreased overall pain levels in participants, and helped them manage pain more effectively

(Kabat-Zinn, 2013). A later study looked at a particular form of mindfulness meditation called *Loving-Kindness* (which you'll be learning more about in the next chapter), and examined its impact on chronic lower back pain. Chronic back pain is an extremely common and often debilitating condition (as I unfortunately know all too well from personal experience). Many forms of treatment tend to be inadequate, resulting in significant ongoing pain as well as psychological distress. As it happens, mindfulness may hold significant promise in helping us manage lower back pain. Participants in a study conducted by James Carson (Carson, 2005) and colleagues at Duke University reported significant decreases in back pain, anger levels, and psychological distress after undergoing *Loving-Kindness* training for a mere eight weeks!

Beyond our immune systems and ability to manage physical pain, mindfulness has been shown to help us in other areas of our health as well. For example, mindfulness has been shown to lead to improved health habits among many people, including promoting more physical exercise and improving sleep (Murphy et al., 2012). It has even been found to be a promising approach when it comes to building healthier eating habits, such as reducing binge-eating and helping to fight against obesity. But it turns out that mindfulness holds great promise in areas even beyond our minds and our physical health.

Mindfulness: Good for Our Lives

At both school and at work, mindfulness offers promising advantages to those who practice it. In the classroom, mindfulness appears to benefit both students and teachers alike. Studies of mindfulness in schools show that students who are taught mindfulness at a young age demonstrate fewer behavioral problems and tend to be less aggressive than their peers. Furthermore, students trained in mindfulness display fewer problems with attention, and even report feeling happier than students not exposed to mindfulness. If you're a teacher reading this, it turns out that mindfulness can help you, too. Teachers who regularly engage in mindfulness practice report lower levels of negative emotion and tend to suffer from lower rates of depression. On a physical level, they even have lower blood pressure readings than their less mindful peers (Flook, 2013).

Stepping outside of the classroom and into the boardroom, the power of mindfulness is no less impressive. Although studies of mindfulness have tended to focus on things like mental and physical health, the past few years have seen an increase in appreciation for the role of mindfulness in the workplace. Although more research is needed, preliminary findings suggest that mindfulness may play an important role in both job performance and job retention (Dane, 2010 & 2013). Specifically, workers who are more mindful tend to display higher job performance on both objective and subjective measures. Moreover, there appears to be an inverse relationship between mindfulness and turnover; in other words, mindful employees are more likely to remain at their job and are more satisfied with their jobs than less mindful workers.

The above findings are striking, but the most important benefit of mindfulness may come in its ability to transform our relationships with those around us. Indeed, one of the most powerful benefits of mindfulness is its impact on both our interpersonal and romantic relationships. In a well-known study on the effect of mindfulness on romantic relationships, researchers found that mindfulness training resulted in higher overall relationship satisfaction, greater closeness, and lower stress level among couples (Carson, 2004). Even more impressively, the results were maintained three months later, suggesting that it's a skill we can continue to benefit from over time.

THE MINDFUL BRAIN

As described above, mindfulness is a skill that can improve our mental health, physical well-being, performance at school or work, and even our relationships. Study after study has shown that the practice of mindfulness can change our lives. But can it also change our brain? Recent evidence suggests that mindfulness can, and does.

When we experience stress or feel upset, our brains respond in a particular and predictable manner. Specifically, fMRI scans show that when we experience distress, the right prefrontal cortex of our brain becomes far more active than the left side (Williams & Penman, 2011; Davidson, 2003). As you'll recall from other chapters, this part of the brain is associated more with negative emotions, whereas the left prefrontal cortex is generally more connected to positive emotions and well-being. In addition to this right-side activation, we also see increased activity in the amygdala, a small almond-sized part of our brain that plays a role in fear activation, arousal, and our fight-or-flight response. So if this is the picture of a stressed brain, what does a mindful brain look like?

When we utilize mindfulness, our brains respond in a very different manner. Rather than seeing this aforementioned right-sided activation, we see increased activity in the left prefrontal cortex (Davidson et al., 2003). This again is the area of our brain more connected with pleasant emotions and positivity. In addition to this, we see *decreased* activity in the amygdala, suggesting that mindfulness can help to reduce our response to threats and enable us to manage stress more effectively (Neff, 2009 & 2011). Furthermore, brain scans reveal increased activity in areas associated with memory, emotion regulation, and learning (Holzel, 2011).

To experience the sorts of changes outlined above, you don't have to practice mindfulness meditation for years, let alone be a Tibetan monk. Rather, many of the findings above were discovered in people who had been trained in mindfulness practice for only a handful of weeks. It's one thing to see temporary changes in brain activation stemming from mindfulness practice. But what about permanent, lasting changes on a structural level in our brain? Can mindfulness actually achieve *that*?

Amazingly, recent research suggests that mindfulness can lead to permanent changes in the structure of our brains over time. When compared to non-meditators, individuals who regularly practice mindfulness have been shown to have increased thickening in parts of the brain associated with attention, concentration and memory, empathy, and decision-making. Beyond that, it even seems that mindfulness can help with the aging process in our brains. We all slowly lose brain cells as we age, a process known as "cortical thinning." Remarkably, studies looking at long-term users of mindfulness show that it seems to slow down and even offset this process. So while we may never find a fountain of youth that keeps us young forever, it seems like mindfulness may be the next best thing!

HOW AND WHY DOES MINDFULNESS WORK?

Mindfulness is an ancient practice, one that has been around for thousands of years. Although originally grounded in Buddhist philosophy, mindfulness has since become widespread, and is now practiced by individuals in all walks of life. As shown in this chapter, mindfulness can lead to powerful changes in our emotional well-being, physical health, and relationship with those around us. But why is mindfulness so incredibly potent? And how can a seemingly simple practice like mindfulness create such remarkable changes across all these areas of our lives? The answers lie in a few areas.

- *Mindfulness changes our brain.* As discussed earlier in this chapter, mindfulness has the power to literally change the structure of our brains. When we practice mindfulness, areas of our brain associated with positive emotion, concentration, and empathy become more activated, while regions associated with stress and fear become inhibited.

- *Mindfulness takes us off autopilot.* All of us are prone to fall into patterns of being on "autopilot" from time to time, whether during our morning commute or as we wash the dishes at night. In small doses this isn't much of a problem, but in larger degrees this habit comes at a cost to our mental and physical health. Mindfulness enables us *to become more present in our day*-to-day lives, and helps us go from a state of mindless autopilot to becoming more fully alive and awakened.

- *Mindfulness changes our relationship to our thoughts.* Our thoughts have a tremendous impact on our mood and mental state. Mindfulness helps in terms of managing negative thoughts in two major ways. First, it enables us to become more aware of negative thought patterns as they emerge, thereby stopping us from spiraling deeper down into depression or anxiety. Second, it enables us to treat our thoughts as mere thoughts, rather than becoming paralyzed and overwhelmed by them. When we come to view a thought as simply a thought, we disarm it rather than buy into it. Over time, mindfulness helps us to become far less troubled and distressed by the thoughts running through our head. The thoughts will still be there, but we come to see them as just that: thoughts, nothing more and nothing less. Or as Jon Kabat-Zinn puts it, "You can't stop the waves, but you can learn to surf."

- *Mindfulness helps put the brakes on rumination.* When we engage in rumination, we obsess over things from the past which cannot be changed, or overthink things in the future which have yet to come. Rumination is a bit like a broken record, where our mind becomes stuck playing the same song over and over again. Although rumination is an unpleasant state, mindfulness holds the power to help break this pattern by bringing us back to the present moment. So rather than incessantly thinking about the presentation we have to deliver at work, or the fight we had last night with our spouse, mindfulness allows us to find peace in the present moment. As Thich Nhat Hanh, the Buddhist monk and author teaches us, "The present moment is filled with joy and happiness; if you are attentive, you will see it."

- *Mindfulness helps us accept reality.* The ancient Chinese philosopher and poet Lao Tzu once wrote, "Life is a series of natural and spontaneous changes. Don't resist them; that only creates sorrow." Modern research confirms this notion, and supports the idea that it is often our resistance to pain, rather than the pain itself, that causes the bulk of our suffering. Like quicksand, the harder we struggle against reality, the more misery we find ourselves immersed in. Mindfulness offers us a different path, and enables us to see and accept reality as it is rather than wish it away. Paradoxically, this sort of acceptance actually enables us to make healthy choices and change our lives.

TIPS FOR PRACTICING MINDFULNESS

In just a few pages, we'll begin reviewing a number of exercises and skills that will enable you to begin incorporating mindfulness into your everyday life. But before doing that, let's first review a few tips and strategies that can help your practice get off the ground:

- *It's OK to keep it short*. Especially when you are starting out, feel free to keep your practice short and sweet. Remember, the most important thing is to begin developing a lifestyle of mindfulness, and there's no wrong place to start. If you can carve out an hour of your day to engage in mindfulness practice, great. But if time is short (which it is in our busy lives), try starting out with ten or fifteen minutes per day and building up from there.

- *Consider both formal and informal practice*. As psychologist Christopher Germer points out, mindfulness can be practiced both formally and informally (Germer, 2009). Formal mindfulness meditation refers to when we allot a certain period of time, say thirty minutes, to formally engage in mindfulness practice. Conversely, informal mindfulness meditation refers to taking small moments, as short as a few seconds throughout the day, to fully notice what's happening around us and within us. Both forms of mindfulness practice can be invaluable, so feel free to experiment with what works best for you and try to incorporate both into your day-to-day life.

- *Be mindful during your "autopilot" activities*. We've discussed how mindfulness can be a powerful antidote against our tendency to drift aimlessly on autopilot. Therefore in some ways, there is no better place to start when it comes to practicing mindfulness. Consider the activities in which you often find yourself daydreaming or mindlessly engaged. These provide us with opportunities to turn mindlessness into mindfulness, and to approach them in a different manner. As Marcel Proust once said, "The real voyage of discovery consists not in seeking out new landscapes, but in having new eyes."

- ***Don't worry about being "good" at mindfulness.*** When we are first learning to practice mindfulness, many of us become stuck worrying about whether we are doing it "right," and can even become frustrated when we feel we aren't doing a "good job" at being mindful. These sorts of judgments can impede us and sabotage our efforts at cultivating mindfulness. When these sorts of thoughts arise, simply notice them and redirect your attention back to the moment.

- ***Consider taking a meditation class.*** This is certainly only an optional suggestion, and many people choose not to do this. Though not a requirement, I can personally attest to the powerful experience of immersing yourself into mindful living through either a formal meditation class or retreat. By enrolling in this sort of experience, you'll find that your skill will accelerate faster and will enable you to harness the many benefits of mindfulness.

- ***Find what works for you.*** The tips outlined above, and the interventions that we'll turn to next, are merely suggestions based on both the latest research on mindfulness as well as my own clinical experience. You, the individual, are the expert on you. Therefore, I invite you to experiment and test out different practices and approaches in order to find the ones that work best for you.

Mindfulness Practices

Mindfulness Practice #1: Mindfulness of the Breath

As we all know from personal experience, our mind has a tendency to wander. As we learned earlier in this chapter, this takes a toll on our mind in the form of increased suffering and unhappiness (Killingsworth & Gilbert, 2010). It's therefore very important to find an anchor, something to center us in the moment in order to come fully into the here-and-now.

Our breath serves as a perfect instrument to accomplish this goal. Our breath is always with us, operating automatically. For 24 hours a day, for every day of our lives, our breath is there like a trusted companion. Wherever we are, and whomever we are with, we can always turn to the breath as a means of grounding ourselves in the present moment. Because of this, our breath will be the focus of our first mindfulness meditation.

Instructions: Begin by finding a comfortable, peaceful place to sit. Set aside around **ten minutes** to start with, though you can extend this as you wish in the days to come. Sit down in a manner that's comfortable, either in a chair or on the ground. Keep your back straight, allowing your shoulders to relax. Close your eyes, or choose a spot on the floor in front of you to focus your gaze.

- **Begin by taking three easy and gentle breaths** in through your nose, followed by slow and steady exhales. With each breath, feel yourself slowing down and becoming more immersed in the moment.

- **If you notice your mind wandering or your thoughts drifting, simply notice this and return your attention and awareness to your breath.** You may notice your mind wandering at many points during this meditation; it's simply what our mind does. Merely observe this tendency, and without judgment, return your awareness to your breathing.

- **Bring full attention now to your breathing.** As you inhale and exhale, observe where in your body you notice your breath the most. Perhaps it's in your chest, as you feel it rise and fall with each breath. Others notice their breath most strongly in their nostrils, as the air passes coolly on the way in, and slightly warmer on the way

(Continued)

out. Still others notice the breath most clearly in their stomach and abdomen, as it rises and falls with each passing breath. Wherever it is, take a moment to simply notice where the breath is most clearly felt in your body.

- **Notice how it feels to fully focus on your inhale.** As you inhale, notice any particular feelings of tension or strain, and notice the sensation of your lungs and abdomen filling up as you inhale.

- **Now gently shift your awareness to focus more on your exhale.** With each exhale, notice what it's like to feel your breath passing out through your nostrils. And observe, without judgment, anything that you feel in your body.

- **For the next few minutes, continue to breathe gently and evenly.** Feel the breath as it comes in through your nose, followed by a steady exhale.

- **Notice what's happening in your mind.** If you notice your mind wandering or your thoughts drifting, don't judge yourself or react self-critically. Simply notice this, and gently redirect your attention and awareness back to your breathing.

- **After ten minutes, gently open your eyes and bring your awareness back to your surroundings.** Allow yourself to bask in the comfort and tranquility of the present moment.

For beginners in mindfulness, this exercise can either be eye-opening or frustrating. You may have noticed your mind becoming flooded with thoughts or judgments, and that's okay. It's our mind's natural tendency to drift and seek out stimulation, and maintaining focused awareness on the breath may feel unnatural initially. But through practice and patience, it becomes easier over time. With practice, you'll even grow to find immense comfort and safety in your breath, which you can turn to whenever you want.

Mindfulness Practice #2: Raisin Meditation

One of the remarkable powers of mindfulness is its ability to transform the mundane into something incredible. We've discussed throughout this chapter our tendency to operate on "autopilot" much of the time, with little conscious awareness of what's happening in the moment. We drive to work, but have little memory afterwards of how we got from "Point A" to "Point B." We read a page in a book, but then have to re-read it because our mind was elsewhere the whole time. And we polish off our favorite meal, only to realize that we barely took time to savor the experience.

In this exercise, we'll harness the power of mindfulness to begin shutting off our autopilot and more fully connecting to the present moment. To do so, we'll start with an activity that all of us do every day: eating. But rather than eating an entire meal in a mindful manner, we're going to start with a much humbler goal – eating a single raisin!

To begin with, set aside around ten minutes of time when you can be undisturbed and alone. You'll need a few raisins for this activity (or if you prefer, any other dried fruit can substitute). In addition, I recommend taking a few moments afterward to write down any reactions you have to the exercise, and what you learned from it.

Instructions: To begin with, take **five to ten minutes** in a quiet place. Ensure that you'll have no distractions; be sure to turn off your phone, shut off the television, and put aside anything else that might take away your attention. For the next few minutes, you'll be doing something that you do every day (eating), but in a different way than usual. Your intention will be to eat a raisin in a mindful manner, fully immersed in the experience.

- **Begin by taking a raisin and placing it in the palm of your hand.** Glance down at it, pretending for a moment that you've never seen anything like it before. Alternate between holding the raisin in your hand, and placing it between your forefinger and thumb to more fully feel its texture. Notice the weight of the raisin as it rests in your hand.
- **Now take a moment to really see the raisin, paying particular attention to its subtle details.** With full attention and awareness, notice the texture of the raisin, and the shadow it

(Continued)

casts on your palm. Notice its ridges, and the particular colors it contains.

- **Placing the raisin between your fingers now,** observe all of its texture with even more awareness. How does it feel to brush your fingers over the raisin? Feel the ridges on its surface.

- **Now bring the raisin up towards your nose.** As you inhale, simply notice any smells or scents that you detect. Or if you cannot detect a scent, simply notice that as well, without judgment.

- **Slowly take the raisin and place it gently in your mouth.** Observe what happens within your mouth when you do; perhaps you'll find yourself salivating, or notice your tongue "reaching out" towards the raisin as you place it in your mouth. Before chewing, simply notice whatever sensations come up in your mouth now that you've placed the raisin on your tongue.

- **Take a single bite into the raisin, and notice how doing so affects your mouth and tongue.** Notice the different textures that you can now pick up on. When you're ready, continue to slowly chew the raisin. But before swallowing, again simply notice all that's occurring right now in your mouth, mind, and body.

- **When you're ready, swallow the raisin,** and continue to observe any feelings, reactions, thoughts, and emotions that come up for you as you do. Without judgment, bring full awareness to whatever is happening inside of you, and take a minute to merely sit with those reactions with your eyes closed.

People have all sorts of reactions to the raisin meditation. For some, it's an eye-opening experience, in that it demonstrates how a simple activity (eating a raisin) can be transformed into something far more meaningful. For others, it feels foreign to eat a raisin in this manner, and can even feel uncomfortable. Whatever your reactions may be, take a moment to simply notice them, and write down some quick thoughts about the exercise:

_____

_____

_____

_____

_____

_____

_____

Mindfulness Practice #3: Everyday Mindfulness

In our last exercise, we discovered how a simple activity (eating a raisin) could be turned into something far more wondrous and meaningful. In this next exercise, we'll take the lessons of the "Raisin Meditation" and apply them to other areas of our lives. Contrast that all-too-common tendency to be mindless as we go about the day with how we cultivated attention and awareness in the "Raisin Meditation." Through simply focusing on what we were doing, our experience was transformed. **And if we can accomplish that through the simple act of eating a tiny raisin, imagine what can happen if we foster that same level of awareness and mindfulness in other areas of our lives.**

Instructions: Begin by reflecting on a handful of activities that you engage in each week, but which you often do in a mindless manner. Common examples include:

- Walking the dog
- Taking a shower
- Brushing your teeth
- Cleaning the sink
- Eating breakfast
- Loading/unloading the dishwasher
- Driving to work
- Walking to the mailbox

For the next week, choose **one** of these activities to focus on each day. You don't have to change the way you do them (such as by slowing down), but rather you'll be changing your level of focus and awareness. **Using the lessons learned from the "Raisin Meditation," engage in one activity each day in a more mindful and present manner.** Use all of your senses to fully engage in the activity, rather than rushing through it or drifting elsewhere in your thoughts. For example, while brushing your teeth you might pay particular attention to the sensation of the toothbrush against your teeth and gums, the flavor of the toothpaste, and how your tongue reacts. You might notice any scents, and observe how your mouth salivates while you brush.

(Continued)

At the end of the week, either in the space below or on a separate piece of paper, write down some reactions to the experience. What was it like to engage in these everyday activities in a more mindful manner? How was it different than usual?

_____

_____

_____

_____

_____

_____

_____

_____

_____

_____

_____

Mindfulness Practice #4: Mindfulness of the Senses

This next mindfulness exercise builds on the "mindfulness of the breath" you practiced earlier, but broadens the practice to increase awareness through our senses. Much like the breath, we can use our various senses (sight, touch, taste, smell, and hearing) to more fully immerse ourselves in the present moment.

Instructions: Begin by finding a comfortable, peaceful place to sit. Set aside around **ten minutes** to start with, though you can extend this as you wish in the days to come. Sit down in a manner that's comfortable, either in a chair or on the ground. Keep your back straight, allowing your shoulders to relax. Close your eyes, or choose a spot on the floor in front of you to focus your gaze.

- **Begin by taking three easy and gentle breaths** in through your nose, followed by slow and steady exhales. With each breath, feel yourself slowing down and become more immersed in the moment.
- **If you notice your mind wandering or your thoughts drifting,** simply notice this and return your attention and awareness to your breath. You may notice your mind wandering at many points during this meditation, it's simply what our mind does. Merely observe this tendency, and without judgment, return your awareness to your breathing.
- **Bring full attention now to your breathing.** Notice the sensation of the breath entering and leaving your body. With each breath, observe yourself becoming more present in the moment.
- **Now shift your attention to the sounds around you.** Notice the sound of your breath, slowly in and slowly out. Notice the sounds around you, even the faintest of sounds. And notice the silence. Imagine your ears as satellites, able to pick up on any sounds around you. Simply notice these things, without judgment, and without any desire for things to be different than they are.
- **Bring your awareness now to any smells you detect.** As you inhale, observe any scents, strong or faint, that your nose picks up on. Again, simply notice this, without judgment.
- **Shift your focus now to feeling your body,** sitting on the floor or on your chair. Notice the weight of your body being supported. Become aware of the fabric of your clothing against your skin, and

(Continued)

the temperature of the air against your skin. Notice your hands, and where they are resting.

- **Now bring your awareness to any tastes** you detect in your mouth. Whether faint or strong, simply observe any tastes that you can pick up on. Or if you cannot, simply notice that as well.

- **With your eyes closed, imagine what the room looks like** around you. Paint a picture in your mind's eye of what surrounds you in this moment. Imagine what's on the walls, and what's at your feet. Visualize the colors of the room where you sit.

- **Now notice what's happening in your mind.** Are your thoughts glancing back towards the past, forward towards the future, or are they here in the present? If you notice your mind wandering or your thoughts drifting, don't judge yourself or react self-critically. Simply notice this, and gently redirect your attention and awareness back to your breathing, and to your senses.

- **After ten minutes, gently open your eyes** and bring your awareness back to your surroundings. Allow yourself to bask in the comfort and tranquility of the present moment.

Mindfulness Practice #5: A Mindful Minute

While I encourage you to try formal meditation practices like the ones presented in this chapter, I also recognize that there are times when life gets in the way. There are some days when even finding ten minutes to set aside for mindfulness is difficult, let alone a half hour. For those occasions, it's useful to take **just a few moments** to cultivate mindfulness and become fully present in the moment. This next exercise invites you to do just that.

Instructions: In our busy world, it's important to take the time to slow down and become one with the present moment. **When you're feeling stressed, try taking a minute to slow down and cultivate mindful awareness.** Whether you are at the office or in your car, and whether you're standing up or sitting down, this exercise can be done virtually anywhere. All you need is a minute of silence. You can close your eyes if you'd like, though you don't have to. For the next minute, put aside whatever you are doing, and focus on the following:

- Feel your breath coming in and out of your nose. Feel your breath as it fills up your chest and lungs, and notice it as it releases on your exhale.

- Use your senses to notice what's happening around you. Hear the sounds around you, and feel the temperature of the air against your skin.

- Observe whatever emotions and thoughts are within you right now. Just notice them, without judgment, and without any desire to change them.

- Notice when your mind drifts, but bring it back each time to your breath.

- When you are ready, open your eyes and come back to the room.

Chapter
7

The Path of Forgiveness

"Resentment is like drinking poison and then hoping it will kill your enemies."

—Nelson Mandela

Inspirational Forgiveness

On February 11th, 1990, the world watched with bated breath as Prisoner Number 46664 was finally released from prison. After 27 years behind bars, and subjected to the harshest of conditions, he strode out from the prison gates and entered a world of freedom. People watched with both curiosity and apprehension, wondering how he would respond. Some worried that he might react with anger, the result of years of pent-up rage. Others feared that the nation would be cast into chaos and bloodshed. The stakes could not have been higher, and it was with this backdrop that Prisoner Number 46664 became a free man. His name: Nelson Mandela.

Imprisoned in 1964 for the "crime" of fighting for freedom and social justice, Mandela had been sentenced to serve his time on Robben Island, a notorious South African prison. Located several miles off the coast of Cape Town, Robben Island is perhaps best compared to Alcatraz in that its proximity to the free world served to only further compound its misery. For days on end, Mandela was forced to chip away at limestone in the scorching hot sun, which resulted in both physical pain and even vision problems that would last the rest of his life. He slept each night on a straw mat, and was confined to a cell barely wide enough to contain his tall frame. During his time on Robben Island, Mandela was permitted to send and receive one letter every six months. His human contact with the outside world was limited to a single thirty-minute visit per year.

Seen in this light, fears of conflict and bloodshed were well founded. After all, anyone subjected to the pain and suffering experienced by Nelson Mandela during those years on Robben Island might be filled with rage and a desire for vengeance. Twenty-seven years had been taken from him, with the prime of his life spent toiling in a limestone quarry and locked behind bars. Now that freedom was finally in his grasp, the world watched in anticipation with a single question on their mind: How would Nelson Mandela respond?

Though revenge and retribution would have been understandable desires, Nelson Mandela chose a different path: the path of forgiveness. Mandela forgave the jailers who had tried to break his spirit. He forgave the South African government who had unjustly robbed him of his freedom. And he forgave the millions of people around the world who had prejudicially cast him as a villain. Several years later when he was elected president of South Africa, Mandela even chose a most unusual guest of honor to help commemorate the occasion: one of his former jailers.

Years later, Mandela reflected on his decision to forgive. Resentment, he realized, would only lead to further pain and suffering. In fact, it would have been as if he never left prison at all. "As I walked out the door toward the gate that would lead to my freedom," he famously stated, "I knew if I didn't leave my bitterness and hatred behind, I'd still be in prison." Hate cannot conquer hate, and so he opted for something different. Mandela would later note that, "People can take everything from you. They can take everything except your mind and your heart. Those things I would have to give them. And I decided not to give them away." Nelson Mandela's decision to forgive enabled him to reclaim his own life and find peace. By extension, his inspirational courage and strength in forgiveness changed the lives of millions of South Africans, and indeed helped make the world a better place.

****

When we are wronged or experience injustice, our impulse is often to respond by fighting fire with fire. We feel pulled to lash back at the person who hurt us, in order to avenge our pain. At other times we may choose instead to avoid the person altogether, yet remain consumed by feelings of anger and resentment. These sorts of reactions are common and understandable. Above all, they are human. And yet there is often an immense cost to these sorts of responses. We can become stuck in bitterness, cling to our feelings of anger, and feel unable to move forward in our lives. In the end, we continue to suffer long after the grievance has passed, harming only ourselves in the process.

As the Buddha said, "Holding onto anger is like grasping a hot coal with the intent of throwing it at someone else. You are the one getting burned."

Forgiveness offers us an alternative path. By letting go of our resentment, and learning to forgive, we can reclaim our lives and rediscover peace and happiness. It is important to remember that forgiveness is in many ways a gift we give ourselves, for no one's sake but our own. We have often heard that forgiveness is a worthy endeavor. Indeed, most major religions around the world posit that forgiveness is a noble pursuit. And many of the greatest thinkers and philosophers throughout history have espoused the value of forgiveness. As the great poet Alexander Pope once wrote, "To err is human; to forgive, divine."

As with many ideas, modern science has only recently begun catching up with these ancient truths. The past decade has seen an explosion of research on the benefits of forgiveness across a range of domains. As it turns out, forgiveness is not merely an honorable pursuit or selfless act. It has actually been shown to be one of the most powerful paths towards achieving happiness and well-being. By choosing forgiveness, we can transform our mental health, physical health, and our lives in a lasting way.

What is Forgiveness?

Forgiveness is a complex topic, and there are many misconceptions out there about the nature of forgiveness. Indeed, of all the paths to happiness featured in this book, I've found that forgiveness can often be the most difficult one for many people to begin implementing. We'll talk in just a bit about what forgiveness is *not*, but first let's try to define forgiveness according to what the latest research says.

Psychologists and other researchers view forgiveness as a conscious effort to let go of anger and resentment towards a person or group who has harmed you. It means liberating ourselves from motivations for revenge or avoidance, regardless of whether or not the other person may deserve it. At times, we may come to replace our negative emotions with more positive attitudes and behaviors; however, the most important step is that we learn to detach from our deeply rooted negative feelings.

Fred Luskin, a psychologist and one of the world's foremost experts on forgiveness, has defined forgiveness as the "experience of peace and understanding that can be felt in the present moment" when we free ourselves from anger and resentment. When we forgive, we come to recognize that "Bad things will not ruin your today, even though they may have spoiled your past" (Luskin, 2002). Luskin emphasizes that even individuals who have experienced great pain and loss are capable of forgiveness.

A crucial aspect of forgiveness to remember is that it is for *you*, not for anyone else. We cannot properly forgive if we are doing it for someone else's sake, or if there are strings attached. True forgiveness entails choosing to let go of the bitterness and resentment we've been holding onto, in order to find happiness and peace. It means taking back the power we've given away, and prioritizing our own healing. Although it's easier said than done, we are all capable of choosing forgiveness. Forgiveness is indeed a difficult process, perhaps the most challenging of all the paths introduced in this book. But if anger and resentment have been holding you back from the life you deserve, forgiveness offers a powerful path to a better future.

WHAT FORGIVENESS IS NOT

When it comes to forgiveness, one of the main roadblocks many people struggle with are the countless misconceptions about forgiveness that we encounter. Many of these involve beliefs that forgiveness will somehow let the other person off the hook, or that it will discount the pain we have suffered with. Although there are too many to list, it's important to review a few of the common misconceptions that can act as barriers in our journey of forgiveness. Here are some things that forgiveness is *not*.

- *Forgiveness is not forgetting.* Despite the old adage that we should perhaps "forgive and forget," true forgiveness does not involve forgetting the pain that we've been caused, or the way we've been hurt. Indeed, we can and should remember what has happened in order to shape our behavior and choices moving forward.

- *Forgiveness is not about the other person.* On the contrary, forgiveness is about you, and your personal choice to release feelings of anger and resentment. Forgiveness is a deeply individual decision, based on your own values, goals, and belief systems.

- *Forgiveness is not condoning or minimizing.* When we forgive another person, we are not condoning their actions, nor are we minimizing the pain we've experienced. Rather, we are choosing to no longer give away space in our mind and hearts "rent-free."

- *Forgiveness is not reconciliation.* Forgiveness may at times be followed by reconciliation, which involves reconnecting with the offender and re-establishing a relationship with them. But at other times, we may appropriately choose to no longer have a relationship with the other person and yet nonetheless forgive them. True forgiveness can and often does occur without the added step of reconciliation.

- *Forgiveness is not a quick fix.* Forgiveness can take time, and there is no set timeframe on the process. In fact, trying to rush through forgiveness can often leave us feeling stuck. By recognizing that forgiveness is a process, we can fully experience our feelings and in time move forward.

These and other misconceptions about forgiveness can hold us back, leaving us stuck and unable to reclaim our lives. As the Chinese proverb reminds us, "Hatred corrodes the vessel in which it's stored." Resentment and anger can indeed corrode us on a psychological and physical level, while forgiveness can offer us a path towards freedom. But before we explore some of the benefits of forgiveness, let's first turn our attention to the ways in which anger and resentment can affect us.

THE HEART OF RESENTMENT

It's been said that in teaching one of his students, the Buddha once asked, "If a person is struck by an arrow, is it painful?" The student reflected on this and affirmed that yes, this would be painful. The Buddha then asked, "Now, if a person is then struck by a second arrow, is it even more painful?" The student again agreed that this would indeed be even more painful. The Buddha went on to explain that in life, we can't control the first arrow, the initial source of our pain. "But the second arrow," he explained, "is our reaction to the first. The second arrow is optional."

Painful experiences are an inevitable part of life. People will hurt us, emotionally or physically. These experiences represent the first arrow, and as long as we are alive we will continue to be struck by these arrows. But the decision to hate, judge, and ruminate represent the second arrow. Whereas the first arrow is often out of our control, the second arrow is self-inflicted. Worse yet, the pain we experience as a result of the second arrow usually far exceeds the first.

When another person hurts us, our initial injury may last seconds or hours. But in our mind, we often continue to replay and rerun the incident for days, months, even years. Like a broken record, our mind remains stuck on the grievance. We want to project our pain back on the person who hurt us, to make them suffer as we have. But no matter how much we fantasize about this, our pain does not lessen. Rather, it becomes amplified.

As we discussed earlier, impulses for revenge or avoidance are entirely natural when we feel wronged or hurt. And indeed, people have many reasons to *not* forgive, including but not limited to:

- Not yet feeling heard or understood
- Not having truly felt the feelings yet
- Not being ready to forgive
- Feeling that the offense is unforgiveable
- Not having processed painful emotions associated with the injury

There are all sorts of reasons we might have to not forgive, and above all forgiveness is a deeply personal choice. But since the aim of this book is to help you achieve greater happiness and well-being in your life, it's worth highlighting the immense ways in which resentment and unresolved anger can stand in the way of this goal. My goal isn't to convince you to forgive if you're not ready, nor is it to suggest that forgiveness is the correct choice in each and every situation. But rather, if resentment or bitterness is getting in your way and stopping you from leading the life you want, I hope to help show you an alternative.

Returning for a moment to the story of the Buddha from earlier, consider for a moment the various "first arrows" you have experienced in your life. These might range from seemingly small offenses (such as someone cutting us off in traffic), to the much larger and more significant (such as being passed over for a work promotion or experiencing cruelty as a child). The "second arrow," in many ways the more painful one, consists of our judgments and anger we have experienced and suffered from as a result of the first. When we excessively focus on our pain and the way we've been wronged, it creates a vicious cycle in which our feelings of anger further deepen. Signs that you have a so-called "second arrow" issue include:

- You find yourself daydreaming or fantasizing about revenge.
- You spend large amounts of time thinking about the painful experience.
- You want to see the other person suffer.
- You feel that you can't achieve real happiness if the other person is around.

- You believe that your life has been ruined as a result of the grievance.
- You experience intense physical reactions (such as muscle tension or increased heart rate) when you think about the person who hurt you.

If you feel that resentment and anger have gotten in the way of your happiness, there is an alternative path: the path of forgiveness. Forgiveness is often thought of as a grand or noble act, a magnanimous and high-minded gesture of compassion that we extend to the person who has hurt us. While there is some truth in these sentiments, it's worth noting that forgiveness can also be viewed through a much more modest and personal lens.

Forgiveness, in short, is good for us, and can help free us from the shackles of resentment and anger which so often keeps us stuck. The past decade has seen an explosion of research on the benefits of forgiveness, and its impact on our emotional and physical well-being. Before we turn our attention to how we can forgive, let's first explore why we even should.

FORGIVENESS: GOOD FOR OUR MINDS

Nelson Mandela once noted that, "Resentment is like drinking poison and then hoping it will kill your enemies." On an anecdotal level, we know this to be true. Indeed, reflect for a moment on a grudge or grievance you have held onto in your own life. Was the other person suffering as a result of your anger and resentment? Of course not. The unfortunate truth is that we are inevitably the one stuck suffering, and not the other way around.

Research confirms this notion, and has highlighted some of the many costs associated with anger and resentment. It turns out that holding onto anger not only feels lousy; it also comes with a host of problems from a mental health standpoint. Indeed, people who hold grudges and find themselves stuck in bitterness perform worse across a number of mental health outcomes. They have higher rates of depression, and report significantly higher levels of stress in their day-to-day lives. They tend to be more anxious in general, and struggle with chronic feelings of anger and hatred. Their overall quality of life, and life satisfaction, tend to be much lower than average.

Forgiveness, on the other hand, is associated with a host of mental health benefits (McCullough & Witvliet, 2001; Luskin, 2002; Worthington, 2007). Individuals who are able to forgive their transgressors report significantly higher levels of well-being, along with lower rates of depression and anxiety. They manage their stress more effectively, and struggle less with anger and neuroticism. Overall, they are much happier, psychologically healthier, and more serene.

Practicing forgiveness doesn't stop us from experiencing heartache and heartbreak. And it doesn't stop us from struggling with pain, anger, or any other negative emotional state. Again, these "first arrows" are a natural and inevitable part of life. Rather, it shows us how to gradually let go of these feelings, in order to reclaim our lives. Forgiveness, in short, shows us how to let go of the "second arrow."

FORGIVENESS: GOOD FOR OUR BODIES

As described above, long-term feelings of anger and resentment are associated with a number of negative mental health outcomes, including depression and anxiety. But worse yet, research has shown that staying stuck in feelings of grievance can wreak havoc on our bodies as well. Indeed, there's now persuasive evidence that holding grudges can be harmful to our physical health.

When we reflect on a grievance, we experience a distinct series of physiological reactions in our body (Witvliet, 2001). Our blood pressure increases, along with our heart rate. Stress chemicals and hormones (such as cortisol) get released, signaling us to spring into action. We sweat more, our muscles tighten, and we experience intense negative emotions. Sound familiar? It's our good old fight-or-flight system revving up. The same physiological cascade that occurs in the face of real danger also rears its ugly head when it comes to thinking about grudges. We might as well have had the grievance just occur, because the feelings remain so intense.

In the heat of the moment, this experience is merely unpleasant. But over time, it can have devastating effects. The sort of chronic stress in our bodies associated with anger and resentment takes an immense toll on our physical health. Our immune system weakens, leaving us more vulnerable to colds and other illnesses. Over time, there's evidence that resentment can increase risks to stress-related health problems including heart attacks. Moreover, there's even some evidence that it can increase our risk of developing cancer (Luskin, 2002).

When we learn to forgive, we are able to put the brakes on this process and can undo the harmful effects stemming from anger and grudges. Almost immediately, our short-term physiological anger reactions (such as increased heart rate and muscle tension) return to baseline. On a chemical level, we see a decrease in cortisol, the stress hormone that has been associated with negative outcomes such as depression, chronic illness, weight gain, and heart disease. By choosing to forgive, we can avoid these and other health problems associated with resentment, and achieve greater health both in our minds and in our bodies.

FORGIVENESS: GOOD FOR OUR RELATIONSHIPS

By definition, forgiveness is an interpersonal endeavor. Perhaps it's not surprising then that many of its most profound benefits are found in our relationships with others. On a direct level, forgiveness holds obvious and powerful benefits in terms of our relationship with the person whom we are forgiving. Whether it's a spouse, coworker, parent, or child, forgiveness enables us to put aside our hurt and begin mending our relationships. Indeed, couples who practice forgiveness report happier relationships and closer bonds, while forgiveness has been shown to help family relationships and friendships alike.

The interpersonal benefits of forgiveness extend far beyond our relationship with the individual whom we are forgiving. Rather, it appears to radiate outwards, improving our relationships with others in our lives, and even with strangers. One well-known study on forgiveness found that an attitude of forgiveness even resulted in people becoming more willing to engage in volunteer work, or donate to charity (Karremans, 2005). Those who forgave even reported feeling more connected to others in their lives, showing that the relationship benefits of forgiveness extend far beyond our relationship with our transgressor. Indeed, forgiveness allows us to find peace from bitterness and resentment, and can often help us rediscover what's most important to us.

YOUR BRAIN ON FORGIVENESS

Many have described the human brain as the "final frontier" of science. Although the past decade has witnessed immense gains in terms of our understanding of the brain, the fact remains that there is still infinitely more that we *don't* know compared with what we know. Even compared to some of the other paths to happiness described in this book (such as mindfulness or gratitude), our understanding of the effects of forgiveness on the brain remains somewhat limited. Nevertheless, the past few years has seen some advances in terms of comprehending what happens in our brain when we forgive.

We discussed some of the powerful physical effects of resentment, including heightened cortisol levels, muscle tension, and increased heart rate. But over the past few years, researchers have been taking things a step further, and have begun examining what happens on a brain-based level when we choose to forgive. In a recent study, participants were asked to imagine a scenario in which another person hurt them (Ricciardi, 2013). They were then asked to envision themselves either forgiving the other person, or harboring anger and resentment towards them. In an added twist, all the participants had to undergo functional magnetic resonance imaging (fMRI) to assess brain activity while they went through these scenarios.

On a subjective level, participants reported feeling much better as a result of the forgiveness condition compared to the resentment condition. They reported lower anger levels, less frustration, and considerable relief when they engaged in forgiveness versus holding onto a grudge. But the brain told an even more powerful story. When participants engaged in forgiveness, an area of the brain called the *inferior parietal cortex* lit up and became more active. This region is strongly connected with empathy, suggesting that forgiveness strategies enable us to feel empathy both for others and ourselves. Another brain area, called the *precuneus*, also became more active as a result of forgiveness. This brain area has been associated with perspective-taking, and being able to put ourselves in other people's shoes. This suggests that a powerful element of forgiveness comes when we learn to see the other person as human, flaws and all, without vilifying them.

Though the science is new, it's an exciting time in forgiveness research. Already, we are gaining hints about how our brain processes forgiveness, which in turn teaches us how to cultivate forgiveness more effectively. The coming years will undoubtedly teach us even more about this life-changing skill.

TIPS FOR PRACTICING FORGIVENESS

If anger or resentment is weighing you down and preventing you from finding happiness, forgiveness is the antidote. Though easier said than done, many people find that forgiveness can be one of the most powerful tools in helping us break free of bitterness and reclaim life. Before we get into some more in-depth techniques to help you in your forgiveness process, feel free to consider the following tips to help you get started:

- *Remember that forgiveness is a process*. Forgiveness takes time, and everyone's pace and progress along their personal journey is different. As clichéd as it sounds, some days will be better than others. Having a day when old feelings of resentment creep up doesn't mean you're backsliding; it simply means you're human.

- *Recognize small milestones*. Along those lines, notice and appreciate signs of progress in your work on forgiveness. When you look up one day and realize that you're not thinking of the old wounds, pat yourself on the back and acknowledge that progress.

- *Get support*. A common barrier to forgiveness occurs when we try to "go it alone." It's crucial to have support from others in order to find peace and forgiveness, and to not try to fight the battle alone. Often by simply feeling heard and understood by another person, we can begin letting go of the old painful emotions.

- *Feel the feelings*. Another common barrier to forgiveness occurs when we haven't properly felt all the feelings associated with our grievance. Oftentimes anger is felt right at the surface, beneath that anger lies pain, sadness, hurt, and grief. It's important to acknowledge and fully feel these underlying emotions, in order to begin truly moving forward.

- *Remember that there are no shortcuts*. Although it might be nice, true forgiveness does not occur quickly or with the snap of a finger. Forgiveness can take time, and trying to bypass steps along the way can leave us feeling stuck.

With those strategies in mind, and armed with knowledge of how forgiveness can transform our lives, let's turn our attention now to a set of practical tools to help you get started on your journey to forgiveness.

Forgiveness Practice #1: The Forgiveness Letter

As we've explored throughout this chapter, holding onto anger and resentment can cause us considerable suffering and emotional pain. It can even harm our bodies, leading to increased stress and a host of physical health problems. The antidote for this, of course, is to choose the path of forgiveness. **Forgiveness can help undo the negative psychological and physiological effects of holding a grudge, and can help us take our power back.** By choosing to forgive, we are able to let go of the pain associated with our interpersonal injury, and return to a life of peace, happiness, and tranquility.

It's important to remember that forgiveness is not about the other person; rather, it's for you and you alone. Moreover, forgiveness does not entail forgetting the offense, or condoning the other person's actions. **In this next exercise, I invite you to write a letter of forgiveness, in order to more fully begin processing your feelings related to the grievance and to begin experiencing the benefits that come with forgiveness.** For this exercise, you will *not* be delivering the letter to the offending party. In addition, I recommend choosing a somewhat lesser offense for your first forgiveness letter, rather than someone who has injured you deeply.

Instructions: Reflect for a moment on people in your life who have hurt you in some way, and who you have never forgiven. Consider the ways in which holding onto your feelings of resentment have affected you over the years. Choose one such individual, and on a separate piece of paper write a brief letter of forgiveness to him/her. In your letter, write a detailed explanation of the way in which you felt hurt by their actions, and how you continue to suffer as a result. Finally, end the letter with an expression of forgiveness towards that person. Let them know that you are choosing to let go of your anger, and to move on with your life. Remember, you do not have to send this letter; this is a step you are taking for you. As such, it can even be written to someone who is deceased. When creating your letter, feel free to consider the following questions to help get you started:

- What did this person mean to you? Were they a stranger or someone whom you were once close with?

  _____

  _____

(Continued)

- How has holding onto the resentment hurt you?

  _____

  _____

- Has anger towards this person prevented you from your own happiness and peace?

  _____

  _____

- How long ago did the offense occur?

  _____

  _____

- How, if at all, has your anger towards the other person impacted their life?

  _____

  _____

Forgiveness Practice #2: Remembering Forgiveness

Choosing to forgive is one of the most challenging of all the paths described in this book. As discussed in this chapter, there are many barriers to forgiveness, ranging from misconceptions about what it means to forgive, to not having properly grieved before preparing to forgive. **If you find yourself feeling stuck and struggling to move towards a place of forgiveness, it can often be helpful to reflect on instances in which we have been on the receiving end of forgiveness.** By doing so, we can begin breaking our own barriers to forgiveness and also gain greater appreciation for the benefits of forgiveness.

Instructions: Take a moment and reflect on a time in which you hurt someone close to you, whether intentionally or not. Perhaps it was by saying something harsh to your family or your significant other, or maybe it was a time when you were insensitive towards a friend. Now choose one of those instances in which the other person chose to forgive you. **Consider what it was like for you to experience their forgiveness, and how it impacted you moving forward.** Close your eyes if it helps, and take a brief moment to fully explore the experience of being forgiven. When you're ready, fill out the following questions about the experience (or use a separate piece of paper):

- Person who forgave you: _____

- How did they convey their forgiveness to you?

  _____

  _____

- How did their forgiveness affect you?

  _____

  _____

- How do you think their choice to forgive might have affected them?

  _____

  _____

- Did your relationship change with the person thereafter?

  _____

  _____

- What can you learn from their decision to forgive?

  _____

  _____

Forgiveness Practice #3: Forgiveness Meditation

This next forgiveness exercise invites you to tap into the **power of meditation** in your journey to forgiveness. For some people, this exercise can initially bring about painful feelings associated with the grievance you have suffered. Yet for many, it can be a valuable experiential exercise to help promote healing. For the purposes of this meditation, choose someone in your life towards whom you continue to harbor anger or resentment. I highly recommend choosing a relatively lesser offense and working your way up from there, rather than starting with someone who has caused you substantial pain. Once you have chosen this individual, use the instructions below to begin your meditation.

Instructions: Begin by finding a comfortable, peaceful place to sit. Sit in a manner that's comfortable, either in a chair or on the ground. Keep your back straight, allowing your shoulders to relax. Close your eyes, or choose a spot on the floor in front of you to focus your gaze.

- **Begin by taking three easy and gentle breaths** in through your nose, followed by slow and steady exhales. With each breath, feel yourself slowing down and becoming more immersed in the moment.
- **If you notice your mind wandering or your thoughts drifting,** simply notice this and return your attention and awareness to your breath. You may notice your mind wandering at many points during this meditation. This is simply what our mind does. Merely observe this tendency, and without judgment, return your awareness to your breathing.
- **Bring full attention now to your breathing.** Notice the sensation of the breath entering and leaving your body. With each breath, observe yourself becoming more present in the moment. Let your mind and body relax and settle into this moment.
- When you are ready, and with your eyes closed, **visualize the person who has hurt you.** As you do, allow yourself to feel the emotions you have been carrying as a result of not forgiving. Continuing to breathe, reflect on the resentment and even anger you have been holding onto.
- **Notice what happens in your mind and your body when you think of this person,** and the pain that they have caused you. You may notice difficult memories coming into your mind, and you might notice your heart rate increase, or your muscles tighten. Strong emotions may start to well up, and that's OK. Let yourself

(Continued)

feel whatever feelings arise. Remind yourself that the pain you feel is a result of both what happened to you in the past, but also your continued carrying of the burden.

- When you feel ready to begin letting go, feel your heart start to open up as you prepare to offer forgiveness to this person who hurt you.
- Say the following out loud:

  "You have caused me hurt and pain, but I have carried this burden for too long. To the extent that I am ready and able, I offer you forgiveness. You have caused me harm, but I forgive you."

- As you continue to breathe, repeat the words "I forgive you" three more times.
- Begin to feel your heart open up further, and notice a weight starting to lift off of you. Slowly feel the painful emotions melt away, and a feeling of calm wash over you.
- As you continue to breathe, feel the burden of bitterness soften, and allow yourself to feel a sense of tranquility pouring over you. For the next minute, simply sit and breathe, allowing these feelings to solidify in your heart.
- When you are ready, open your eyes and return fully to the room.

Forgiveness Practice #4: Drawing Strength from Adversity

As many of us know from personal experience, it can be all too easy to become stuck in a downward spiral after someone close to us causes us pain. Whether we are hurt by infidelity, a cruel comment from our boss, or pain inflicted by a family member, it is easy to find ourselves stuck in feelings of anger and resentment. Worse yet, these feelings can fester, causing us pain for months or even years after the incident occurred.

Although it may seem counterintuitive, much research suggests that an important way to cope with these feelings is to shift our focus away from the pain we have suffered. As an alternative, we can instead choose to focus on the *good* things that resulted from what happened to us. Even in the case of traumatic experiences, research has shown that writing about benefits that occurred as a result of the trauma can help people build meaning from their experience and move forward with their lives (King & Miner, 2000). According to this research, writing about the ways in which we grew or transformed after our painful incident can help us push through our pain and come out stronger for it.

Over time, this shift in focus can help lay the groundwork for us to let go of our anger and resentment and forgive more fully. Most importantly, we can come to see that we are not damaged or broken as a result of the pain inflicted on us; rather, we can even become stronger for it. For this next exercise, think about someone who has hurt you, and whom you continue to hold anger towards. As with prior exercises, it's better to choose someone who has perpetrated a more minor offense to begin with, and progressively work our way up from there.

Instructions: Find a quiet place to sit and reflect. Begin by thinking about a person who has harmed you in some way, whether emotionally or physically. The incident should be from the past, and <u>not</u> an ongoing offense. Reflect on what the person did to you, and how they hurt you. Consider how you have held onto anger and resentment towards them. Reflect on how long you've held this grudge, and how your life has been impacted as a result. **When you are ready, on a separate piece of paper, spend the next fifteen minutes writing only about the positive things that have occurred as a result of the experience.** This might seem difficult at first, but think long and hard, looking deep in your heart. Consider the ways in which you have grown from this experience, how you have changed as a result of it, and how have even become stronger from it. If you are struggling, consider the following questions to prompt you:

(Continued)

- Have you grown in some way as a result of what happened?
  _____
  _____

- Have you learned anything about yourself because of the incident?
  _____
  _____

- Have you grown closer with anyone as a result of the offense?
  _____
  _____

- Have you learned who you can turn to in times of need?
  _____
  _____

- Do you have a greater sense of personal value?
  _____
  _____

- Do you have a clearer sense of your own needs and values?
  _____
  _____

- Are you more able to appreciate anything since the incident?
  _____
  _____

- Have you become more self-reliant?
  _____
  _____

- Have you become more empathic and compassionate towards others?
  _____
  _____

Forgiveness Practice #5: Empathize

We've all been hurt at some point in our lives. We've been treated poorly, experienced rejection, and had our hearts broken. The pain we experience in these moments is normal, and entirely human. But all too often, the pain lingers and remains with us for months, or even years. It stays with us, causing us further pain and heartache long after the offense was committed.

The alternative is to choose forgiveness. But forgiveness is difficult, in part because our anger leads us to view the other person as our enemy, and to blame them entirely for our feeling. **A precursor to forgiveness, therefore, can be to cultivate empathy for the person who hurt us.** Depending on the nature of the offense, it can help to put ourselves in the other person's shoes. This doesn't mean that we agree with, condone, or validate their actions. But rather, empathizing with them allows us to see the other person as a human being, flaws and all, rather than our adversary. **Once we achieve greater understanding of the other person, we become more able to forgive.**

This next exercise invites you to cultivate the power of empathy and compassion, even towards people who have caused us pain in the past. As always, I recommend starting with someone who committed a somewhat less egregious offense, and then working your way up from there.

Instructions: Take a moment and reflect on an ongoing resentment that you carry towards another person. Think about the way in which this person hurt you and the way you felt as a result of their actions. Notice the emotions that come up for you as you think about them, and consider whether you are ready to begin the process of letting go. **When you feel ready, try to put yourself in the other person's shoes.** Think about the offense they committed, and reflect on why they might have acted as they did. Try and work from an assumption that this person made a mistake, but that they did not act out of evil or malice. Close your eyes and open your heart, continuing to reflect on this issue. If it helps, feel free to use the following questions to guide your process:

- How might they explain what happened, from their point of view?

  _____

  _____

(Continued)

- What was their upbringing like?

  _____

  _____

- How might their own past experiences have led them to behave this way?

  _____

  _____

- Could they have meant something different by what they said or did?

  _____

  _____

- Have I ever made a similar mistake?

  _____

  _____

- Did I play any role in what happened?

  _____

  _____

- How might forgiveness help this person?

  _____

  _____

- How might forgiveness help me?

  _____

  _____

Chapter 8

The Path of Self-Compassion

"Love yourself first, and everything else falls in line. You really have to love yourself to get anything done in this world."

—Lucille Ball

THE SCARS THAT REMAIN

The war had been over for more than two decades, and his physical wounds had long since healed over. But for Richard Luttrell, the emotional scars of Vietnam continued to haunt him. In some respects, and certainly from the outside, he seemed to have fully moved on. He had gotten married, fathered children, and built a successful career. In his spare time, Richard enjoyed fishing and was an avid skydiver. Yet for years something gnawed at him, an echo of the past from which he could not free himself.

Decades earlier, when he was just eighteen years old, Richard had volunteered to serve his country in the Vietnam War. The war was starting to escalate, and he had been deployed halfway around the world to a place many Americans would have had trouble locating on a map. It was early in his deployment, and he had not yet experienced combat, let alone seen the enemy face to face. Then one day, while slogging up a treacherous trail in a mountainous region called Chu Lai, Richard's life would forever change.

Out of the corner of his eye, he spotted a North Vietnamese soldier just a few yards away, aiming an AK-47 rifle directly at him. Richard looked up, fear rushing over him, and he froze. For a few moments, but what felt like hours, the two men locked eyes in the jungle. The soldier stood there, gun aimed, but he did not fire. With death staring him in the face, Richard suddenly reacted out of instinct and fired his own weapon at the soldier. The sound of gunshots shattered the silence of the jungle, and the North Vietnamese soldier fell to the ground.

The enormity of the situation soon began to hit him. Richard was struck by the reality that his own life could have easily ended moments before, and that he had just taken a life in order to save his own. He wondered why the other man didn't shoot, why he had just stood there in silence. It was at this moment that Richard noticed something. It was a small detail, one that could have quite easily been overlooked. As he looked down upon his fallen foe, he noticed a tiny photograph lying on the ground beside him.

The small photograph showed a soldier next to a girl. He recognized the soldier as the man he had just slain. The girl looked young, perhaps seven or eight years old, and both looked forward towards the camera with sad eyes, the sort of eyes you'd expect when saying goodbye. To this day, Richard Luttrell cannot say what compelled him to pick it up. But he did, and for years he couldn't let go.

Richard came home after the war and was greeted by medals and commendations. He married his high school sweetheart, and soon they started a family. But part of him could never leave that day in the jungle, nor could he forget the images from that tiny photograph. For over twenty years he carried the image in his pocket, a constant reminder of life's fragility and preciousness. Richard grew to feel a strange sense of connection and kinship to the figures in the picture. And yet he was also tormented by immense guilt over what he had done. "Here's a young daughter who doesn't have a father thanks to me," he would later reflect.

Richard carried his guilt for decades, until one day he found himself on a family vacation in Washington, DC. While visiting the Vietnam Veterans Memorial, he decided that he had carried the burden for long enough. In his heart, he knew it was time to let go, and so he wrote a letter to his fallen foe and left it along with the picture at the Memorial. In his letter, Richard apologized for taking the man's life, for leaving his daughter without a father, and expressed admiration for the man's courage. But he also signaled a readiness to forgive himself, and to release the chains of the past. "It is time for me to continue the life process, and release the pain and guilt. Forgive me," he wrote. And with that, Richard Luttrell had let go of his innermost demons.

Richard Luttrell's story of self-forgiveness and redemption would have been inspiring and uplifting enough had it ended there, but he had one more journey to make. Several years later, through a fellow veteran who had heard about his tale, the photograph had miraculously made its way back to Richard. He now knew what he had to do. Richard traveled to Vietnam and was able to track down the young girl from the photo, now a grown woman. He introduced himself, and tearfully asked her for forgiveness while returning the photograph to her. The woman herself burst into tears, and embraced Richard tenderly. Later, she would explain that she and her family had long believed that her father's spirit had lived on in Richard. That day, when Richard returned the photograph, her father's spirit had returned too.

****

Do you treat yourself as well as you treat your friends and family? When things go wrong, do you tend to react with self-criticism and judgment? These sorts of questions tap into the notion of *self-compassion*, a growing area of research in the field of psychology. For many of us, it's much easier to treat others with kindness and caring in times of need, whereas we often treat ourselves with harshness. We believe that self-criticism will somehow spur us into action, motivate us to do better next time, and help us to overcome our human imperfections. But research indicates that the opposite is in fact true. Rather than motivate us towards improvement, self-criticism demoralizes us and can even prevent us from achieving our goals.

On the other hand, a growing body of research now suggests that treating ourselves with kindness and compassion is in fact crucial for achieving lasting happiness and well-being. Ancient wisdom from the East has long espoused this view, and has stressed the importance of self-compassion in our lives. Indeed, Buddhist philosophy has long held that learning to care for oneself is even necessary before one can offer compassion and care to others. In recent years, Western psychology has begun to catch up to these long-held truths. Self-compassion is now considered a key ingredient in helping us achieve a life of happiness and contentment. Most importantly, self-compassion is a skill that any of us can learn to grow and cultivate within us, in order to lastingly change our lives.

SELF-COMPASSION VERSUS SELF-ESTEEM

In 1990, the California State Legislature released a long-anticipated report entitled "Toward a State of Esteem." The idea was both well intentioned and bold. Through teaching self-esteem in the classroom, the theory went, children could become "immunized" against a host of problems later in life. From unwanted pregnancy, to drug use, and even suicide, the self-esteem movement (which had been building for more than two decades) aimed to reverse these social ills through helping children achieve a greater sense of self-worth. At the time, this seemed like a great idea. After all, who wouldn't want to have higher self-esteem? There was only one problem: It resulted in few, if any, meaningful gains in any of these areas. In fact, the focus on self-esteem as a "be all, end all" ended up even having some unexpected negative consequences.

Despite the failure of the California report, the emphasis on self-esteem remains a remarkably powerful and alluring prospect for most people. If you walk into your local bookstore, you'll see dozens of new titles espousing the benefits of self-esteem, and purporting to show you how to achieve it. On Amazon there are literally thousands of books on the topic of self-esteem, promising to guide you to a path of joy and success by learning to boost your self-worth. On the surface, this all makes sense. Who wouldn't want to like themselves a bit more? But digging a little deeper, some troubling signs emerge.

The main problem, as it turns out, isn't necessarily with self-esteem itself. To summarize, self-esteem refers to our general sense of self-worth, how much we like ourselves, and our overall value as a person. Having high self-esteem has often been connected to positive psychological outcomes, whereas low self-esteem is replete with negative states like depression and low motivation.

But significant problems emerge as a result of our constant *emphasis and pursuit* of self-esteem, and our incessant quest to boost feelings of self-esteem. In general, because self-esteem is so closely connected to things like accomplishments and the perceptions of those around us, we are left with two general ways we can boost our self-worth at any given time either by elevating and "puffing up" ourselves, or by putting down those around us. Neither road leads to a good place.

According to many social scientists, one of the problems with our focus on self-esteem is that it leads to a sense of "contingent self-worth." In other words, when we do well in life, we feel good about ourselves and our self-esteem shoots up. But when we experience setbacks or feel like we aren't quite measuring up, our self-esteem goes in the tank. For many of us, self-esteem becomes inherently tied up with whether we feel successful or not, beautiful or not, or receive approval or not from those around us. Our quest for self-esteem often leads to a number of unintended negative consequences, such as self-criticism, alienation from others, self-absorption or narcissism, and a fragile sense of self when we experience setbacks. Self-esteem is an inherently unstable concept, a rollercoaster that can lead us to great heights but also tremendous depths. But is there another way?

According to the latest research, self-compassion offers the same benefits as self-esteem without the negative drawbacks (Germer, 2009; Neff, 2011).

Rather than being dependent on external validation or accomplishments, self-compassion allows us to connect with ourselves in a more human and gentle manner. The good feelings that come along as a result of self-compassion are far more stable and can remain even during times of hardship and setbacks. When we are self-compassionate, we don't need to feel better than others in order to feel good about ourselves; rather, we are able to care for ourselves and treat ourselves with the sort of kindness we all deserve.

WHAT IS SELF-COMPASSION?

Think about the last time you suffered a setback, or a time when you felt as if you didn't "measure up." Perhaps it was an incident at work, a conflict at home, or not performing well on a test at school. Do you remember how you responded? Can you recall how you spoke to yourself in the aftermath of what happened?

If you're like many people, you might have responded with self-criticism or shame, berating yourself for your perceived shortcomings. "What's the matter with me?" or "Why can't I handle this?" are common refrains in our internal dialogue. We believe that by responding in this manner, we'll somehow spur ourselves to action and do better the next time. But this belief turns out to be misguided. Rather than motivate us towards positive change, self-criticism ends up demoralizing us over time. It compounds our misery, and lowers our sense of self-worth. Yet this pattern remains deeply ingrained in many of us, and is only reinforced by many of the cultural messages we receive. Is there an alternative?

This is where self-compassion comes in. Rather than incessantly labeling ourselves as good or bad, self-compassion offers us a different path. According to Kristin Neff, one of the foremost researchers in the field, self-compassion enables us to "stop judging and evaluating ourselves altogether" (Neff, 2011). At its core, self-compassion allows us to treat ourselves with the same degree of kindness we might offer a close friend, or even a stranger. For many of us, it's far easier to offer support to those around us than it is to turn that kindness inwards towards ourselves. But recent findings suggest that learning to do so is imperative when it comes to boosting our happiness and well-being.

We are all familiar with the concept of compassion, which refers to the feelings that arise when we notice another's suffering and feel moved to relieve their pain. The word compassion stems from the Latin roots *com* (meaning "with") and *pati* (meaning "suffer"). Compassion therefore literally means to suffer together, or to suffer with, one who is in pain. By extension, when we cultivate *self-compassion*, we turn this process of compassion inwards and learn to foster kindness and caring towards ourselves.

As defined by Neff, self-compassion consists of three distinct yet interconnected components: self-kindness, common humanity, and mindfulness (Neff, 2011). *Self-kindness* refers to the importance of being gentle with ourselves and understanding of our own shortcomings. Rather than respond with harshness or criticism in the face of setbacks, self-kindness emphasizes that we treat ourselves with compassion and acceptance. The second component of self-compassion, *common humanity*, denotes the feeling of being connected with others rather than feeling isolated and alone as a result of our suffering. We become able to recognize that feelings of pain and disappointment are universal, and that we are not solitary in our struggles. It is this aspect of self-compassion that helps distinguish it from self-pity. Finally, *mindfulness* refers to non-judgmental awareness and acceptance of the present moment. Rather than anxiously glancing towards the future, or ruminating about the past with regret, mindfulness allows us to find peace and understanding in the present.

According to the latest research, it is necessary to incorporate all three of these elements in order to reap the full benefits of self-compassion. By learning to be kinder to ourselves, accepting our limitations, and treating ourselves the way we treat others, we come one step closer to lasting feelings of well-being and happiness. Yet despite these promises, the concept of self-compassion is often met with resistance. In my experience, part of this is due to common misconceptions about the nature of self-compassion, which we'll turn our attention to now.

BARRIERS TO SELF-COMPASSION

As reviewed in the last section, self-compassion refers to the concept of becoming kinder to ourselves, and learning to treat ourselves with the same sort of respect and compassion we would give a friend or loved one. Its three core components (self-kindness, common humanity, and mindfulness) must be combined in order for us to fully reap the benefits of self-compassion. But equally important to defining self-compassion is clarifying what it is *not*. Indeed, in my clinical work with patients, self-compassion can often be one of the most challenging concepts to internalize, largely due to some common misconceptions about it.

Many individuals have some initial hesitancy or pushback when it comes to working on self-compassion. Common concerns I often encounter include fears that self-compassion will lead to undesirable outcomes like complacency, or lead people to lose their "edge." Others express reservations that self-compassion will lead them to rest on their laurels, or promote self-pity during times of struggle. So before we delve further into the benefits of self-compassion and how to enhance it, let's first dispel some common myths when it comes to self-compassion. Remember, self-compassion is *not*:

- *Selfish.* On the contrary, by learning to love and care for ourselves, we actually become *more* able to give to others. As Buddhist author and teacher Jack Kornfield points out, "If your compassion does not include yourself, it is incomplete."

- *Positive Affirmations.* Oftentimes, daily affirmations can feel trite or clichéd, like a real-life version of Stuart Smalley from *Saturday Night Live*. True self-compassion, on the other hand, isn't about fooling ourselves; rather, it comes from a genuine place of caring and thoughtfulness.

- *A Pity Party.* Acknowledging our pain and offering compassion to ourselves is not akin to wallowing or complaining. In fact, by facing our struggles with an open heart and clear eyes, we actually become more able to pull ourselves out of despair and move forward in our lives.

- *Glossing over reality.* Some people fear that self-compassion will lead us to sugarcoat or gloss over painful realities in our lives. On the contrary, it enables us to see reality clearly, with kindness and concern, and enables us to experience life in a more genuine and full manner.

In addition to the myths and misconceptions outlined above, culture plays a large role in either promoting or discouraging self-compassion. Here in the United States, along with many Western nations, self-compassion is often seen as contrary to our cultural values of independence and individual success. Self-criticism is all too common, and is seen as a source of motivation to help spur us towards self-improvement.

Interestingly, Confucian-influenced cultures such China and Taiwan seem to share many of these same tendencies and may have even lower levels of overall self-compassion than the United States (Neff, 2003). However, in countries influenced more by Buddhism, self-compassion rates tend to be much higher, while rates of self-criticism appear much lower. And across all cultures, it appears that high levels of self-criticism are connected to depression and poor life satisfaction, whereas the reverse is true of self-compassion.

SELF-COMPASSION: GOOD FOR OUR MINDS

From a mental health standpoint, self-compassion has been shown to possess powerful benefits, as well as offering significant protective factors against mental health problems. In her book entitled *Self-Compassion*, Dr. Kristin Neff reviews many of the exciting benefits of this skill. One of the most consistent and reliable findings in the literature is that individuals who are high in self-compassion tend to have significantly lower rates of depression and anxiety (Neff, 2011). Moreover, the relationship between these factors does not appear to be merely correlational, but rather causal. Indeed, studies have shown that our level of self-compassion may account for as much as half of the variation in our depression or anxiety levels. By extension, we can infer that by cultivating self-compassion, we are able to buffer and protect ourselves from falling into episodes of depression or anxiety.

Even in the most trying of circumstances, self-compassion offers hope. In one study, researchers looked at individuals who had experienced a traumatic event, such as a rape or a car accident (Thompson & Waltz, 2008). First, they assessed for symptoms of posttraumatic stress disorder (PTSD), a severe anxiety disorder triggered by significant traumas like those just mentioned. Common features of PTSD include symptoms such as re-experiencing the traumatic event (such as through flashbacks or nightmares), disturbed sleep, heightened anxiety, increased arousal, and persistent fear. Second, the researchers looked at how self-compassionate the participants were. Interestingly, they found that self-compassion had an inverse relationship with symptoms of PTSD. Meaning, the higher a person was in terms of self-compassion, the less severe their symptoms of PTSD tended to be.

SELF-COMPASSION: GOOD FOR OUR BODIES

If you're one of many Americans who suffer from chronic pain, you'll be pleased to know that self-compassion has been shown to alleviate many forms of chronic pain, including lower back pain. Better yet, you don't have to practice for years in order to reap these benefits; rather, some studies show that as little as eight weeks can do the trick. In one well-known study, researchers trained individuals with chronic lower back pain in a particular form of meditation designed to enhance compassion to oneself and others, referred to as *Loving-Kindness*. After a mere eight weeks, participants who engaged in this practice reported significantly lower levels of back pain, and were better able to cope with their injuries (Carson, 2005).

Self-compassion can also help us in terms of our eating, helping to promote healthier habits when it comes to food. In a fascinating study, researchers looked at the impact of self-compassion on how individuals responded to lapses in their diet (Leary & Adams, 2007). In other words, they looked at what happened when people slip up and eat a "forbidden" food (like pizza or a donut) when they are trying to eat a healthier diet. Many of us in that situation might respond with self-criticism, believing that this will whip us back into shape and help us get back on track.

But the opposite seems to be true. According to this study, self-compassionate individuals responded to lapses with less criticism, and were actually *less* likely to lapse again. In other words, by treating themselves gently rather than harshly, the participants were more able to get themselves on track and continue eating in a healthy manner. Learning to treat ourselves with kindness appears to help with a number of other physical issues, including chronic acne believe it or not. In a compelling study, researchers demonstrated that self-compassion was strongly connected to lower stress levels among individuals suffering from chronic acne issues (Kelly et al., 2009). Perhaps most amazingly, they not only reported lower levels of psychological distress stemming from their acne, but also endorsed reduced physical symptoms such as itching and scratching. Self-compassion, it seemed, not only helped the mind in this instance but the body as well.

When it comes to reducing or eliminating unhealthy behaviors, it appears that self-compassion holds promise in this area as well. In one recent study, researchers examined the impact of self-compassion on cigarette smoking (Kelly et al., 2010). Though all of the participants in the study reported feeling motivated to quit smoking, those who were trained in self-compassion were able to reduce their daily cigarette use much more rapidly than the comparison group of participants. Again, it appears that by reducing self-criticism and learning to treat themselves with kindness and compassion, individuals in this study were more able to meet their goals and achieve greater health.

SELF-COMPASSION: GOOD FOR OUR LIVES

Some of the most powerful benefits of self-compassion consist of the changes we experience in our relationships with others. Studies suggest that self-compassion helps foster feelings of closeness and interpersonal connection, as opposed to self-criticism, which serves to distance us from others (Germer, 2009). Self-compassionate individuals are also more able to foster authentic and close interpersonal relationships than those who tend more towards self-criticism. According to one study, individuals who are more self-compassionate are also able to turn that compassion outwards towards others. They focus more on offering help and encouragement to friends, and tend to be more patient and understanding of others' mistakes (Crocker & Canavello, 2008). In romantic relationships, self-compassion also allows us to be more accepting, nurturing, and supportive towards our partners (Neff, 2011).

Self-compassion also appears to help us at work and at school. As discussed earlier in this chapter, we often react to setbacks or failure with self-criticism, believing that this will somehow spur us towards improvement. But the research suggests that quite the opposite is true. Self-criticism wears us down, and demoralizes us over time. On the other hand, self-compassionate people are better equipped to cope with setbacks, and actually end up achieving greater success in school and in the workplace (Neff, 2011). So in life, as in love, it helps to be self-compassionate.

Your Brain on Self-Compassion

The benefits of self-compassion are vast, but a closer look at some of the brain chemistry behind the practice provides clues about its power. The research is still evolving, and the coming years will undoubtedly be an exciting time as we continue to learn more about the brain changes that result from increased self-compassion. But there are already some hints about what happens to our brain when we cultivate self-compassion.

Before turning our attention to self-compassion however, it's informative to explore a bit of what happens when we're self-critical. When we engage in self-criticism, a particular area of the brain referred to as the amygdala becomes more activated. As you'll recall from other chapters, the amygdala is a small almond-shaped region of the brain responsible for (among other things) our fight-or-flight response. When our amygdala lights up, it triggers this fight-or-flight response, including increased blood pressure along with releasing high amounts of adrenaline and cortisol (a stress hormone) into our bloodstream.

In addition, we see increased activity on the right prefrontal region of our brain, an area associated with negative emotional states. This sort of brain state is entirely normal and adaptive when we're confronted with real danger; however, a significant problem arises when it becomes the norm for us. Over time, the processes outlined above lead to a host of difficulties including chronic stress and exhaustion. So clearly, long-term self-criticism takes a toll on our mind and body. But what about self-compassion?

When we foster self-compassion, our brains respond in a very different manner. Studies show that there are two areas of the brain in particular that are impacted by self-compassion: the left prefrontal cortex and the insula. These areas of the brain are strongly connected to positive emotions, such as peace, tranquility, and happiness. By increasing activation in these areas, we are doing our part in wiring our brain for happiness and well-being.

In addition to brain activation, self-compassion also appears to lead to hormonal changes as well. For example, some studies suggest even brief exercises designed to boost self-compassion can result in decreased levels of cortisol in our bodies. In addition, research suggests that self-compassion may lead to increased levels of oxytocin, a hormone closely connected with love and bonding. Higher levels of oxytocin have been connected to feelings of trust, calm, safety, and connection. Though usually activated interpersonally, it is thought that the same process occurs when we turn kindness in towards ourselves as well.

SUMMING UP

Despite a longstanding emphasis on self-esteem as the "be all, end all," it appears that self-compassion offers all the same benefits as self-esteem without its considerable drawbacks. Indeed, self-compassion has been shown to have a powerful effect on our minds, our bodies, our relationships, and our performance at work or at school. Most exciting of all, self-compassion is a learnable practice. While it may come more naturally to some than others, all of us can learn to become more self-compassionate in order to reap the benefits of this valuable practice. Let's now turn our attention to some proven ways to increase self-compassion in our lives.

SELF-COMPASSION PRACTICES

Self-Compassion Practice #1: A Letter of Self-Compassion

In this first exercise, you'll begin exploring how to build self-compassion when it comes to areas of your life you normally criticize. **To help you do so, you'll envision yourself receiving kindness and compassion from someone you love and trust.** Drawn from the work of psychologist Kristin Neff, this exercise can be a powerful jumping-off point for many people in their path to increased self-compassion.

__Instructions:__ We all have things about ourselves that we don't like, or that we tend to criticize. These might include something about the way we look, how we perform at work, or how we are around others. These feelings of inadequacy are painful indeed, but are an inevitable part of life for all of us. Take a moment and reflect on <u>one</u> of these aspects of yourself that you often fixate on in a negative way. Feel whatever emotions come up for you and notice the sorts of judgments that arise in your mind when you reflect on this issue.

Next, think about someone in your life who is kind, caring, loving, and compassionate towards you. It can either be a real person with whom you feel closeness and trust, or if you prefer, someone you imagine. This person can see your best qualities, as well as your areas of weakness. They understand and care for you, in good times and in bad. They understand that you are a human being, with strengths as well as flaws. Above all, they accept you and love you unconditionally, imperfections and all.

For the next few minutes, on a separate piece of paper, write a letter to yourself from the point of view of this friend. Focus in particular on the issue you came up with earlier, whether it was something to do with appearance, career success, or how you are in a particular relationship. What might this friend say to you regarding your perceived flaw or failure? How might they offer you comfort and demonstrate caring towards you? What might they do to show you kindness and compassion? How might their voice sound? What feelings would they want to convey towards you? Imagine this scenario, and allow yourself to feel whatever emotions come up.

When you are ready, fill your letter with the sense of compassion and love that this friend has for you. Once you have finished writing it, re-read the letter to yourself, letting the words sink in. Close your eyes, and feel the warmth and compassion flowing over you. Feel it growing and welling up inside of you. It is yours now, an infinite and renewable source of love and support, here for you whenever you need it.

Self-Compassion Practice #2:
Loving-Kindness Meditation

Earlier in this chapter, we briefly discussed a particular form of meditation called Loving-Kindness. Loving-Kindness, also known as *Metta*, is a practice that dates back to at least the fifth century. While the mindfulness meditations taught earlier in this book tended to primarily emphasize attention and awareness, **Loving-Kindness is instead aimed at cultivating connection.** Using words, emotions, and images, Loving-Kindness has the power to instill deep feelings of love, compassion, and happiness within us.

Though it dates back over a thousand years, Loving-Kindness has grown tremendously in popularity in recent years. Along with this influx of public interest, there has also been increased academic attention being paid to this form of meditation. In recent years, researchers have discovered numerous benefits that stem from regular practice of Loving-Kindness, including **improved mental health, better physical health, and even changes to our brain.** It even reduces inflammation in our body, and improves our overall response to stress.

Although the complete version of Loving-Kindness often includes shifting our attention outwards towards others in our lives, for the purposes of this exercise we will keep our attention focused within us. Drawn from the work of psychologist Christopher Germer (2009), this exercise can help form part of your foundation of self-compassion. Set aside ten or fifteen minutes per day to begin this practice initially, though over time you may choose to increase this timeframe.

Instructions: Begin by sitting in a comfortable position. Sit upright and relaxed, with your hands resting on your lap. Take three steady and even breaths, and when you are ready, close your eyes.

- Continue to breathe, slowly in and slowly out. Notice the feeling of the air entering through your nose, and observe how it's slightly warmer on the way out.
- Become aware of your body as you sit. Feel your body as it makes contact with the support beneath you. Feel your body resting comfortably, and notice any sensations within your body.
- When you are ready, form an image of yourself in your mind's eye. Picture yourself as you currently sit, and feel your heart open up.

(Continued)

Remind yourself that like anyone else, you wish to live happily and in peace. Connect fully with that intention, and feel a sense of warmth and compassion pour over you.

- Continue to picture yourself as you sit in this moment. Gently and in silence, repeat the following phrases to yourself:

May I be safe.

May I be happy.

May I be healthy.

May I be peaceful and at ease.

- Take your time, all the while maintaining the image of yourself in your mind's eye. Allow the feelings of peace and tranquility to sink in, and savor the meaning of the words.

- When you notice your mind wander or your thoughts drift, simply notice this, and return to the present moment.

- Repeat the phrases a second time, again gently and in silence:

May I be safe.

May I be happy.

May I be healthy.

May I be peaceful and at ease.

- Once more, fully allow the words to sink in, and feel your heart open up with love and compassion towards yourself. Take a moment to savor this moment.

- When you are ready, gently open your eyes and return to the room.

Self-Compassion Practice #3:
Seeing the Double Standard

For many of us, it's far easier to treat others with kindness than it is to treat ourselves in the same way. But as we've learned throughout this chapter, it's absolutely crucial to our well-being to learn how to do so. Indeed, the latest findings in the area of self-compassion suggest that true happiness lies in being able to treat ourselves with the same degree of kindness and compassion that we offer so freely to those around us. As author Louise Hay reminds us, "you have been criticizing yourself for years, and it hasn't worked. Try approving of yourself and see what happens." In this next exercise, you'll be exploring the differences between how you treat yourself versus the way you treat those closest to you.

Instructions: Take a moment and think about a close friend or family member who means a great deal to you. Reflect on who this person is to you, and how much you care for them. Allow yourself to fully feel the sense of closeness and connection that you have with this person, and get in touch with the warm, positive feelings you hold for them. **Once you have done so, take a separate piece of paper and briefly respond to the following questions:**

1. Imagine that this friend is struggling with a particular issue, and is suffering in a significant way. How might you come to their aid? How would you respond to this person in their time of need? Briefly write down what you might say or do, and the manner in which you would do so.

2. Now reflect on times in your life when you have struggled and found yourself suffering in a significant way. How did you respond? How do you tend to react towards yourself in these sorts of situations? Briefly write down what you tend to say to yourself in these instances, and how you tend to respond to your own times of need.

3. What differences did you notice when comparing the way you treat yourself with the way you treat others? Do you tend to be kinder towards those around you than you are to yourself? How do you think your life might be different if you learned to treat yourself with the same degree of compassion?

Self-Compassion Practice #4: Self-Appreciation

As many of us know, it is often far easier to focus on our weaknesses than our strengths. There are of course many reasons for this, including but not limited to our brain's built-in negativity bias that we discussed earlier, as well as the widespread belief that self-criticism will somehow motivate us to greater heights. In addition, for both cultural and societal reasons, many of us are uncomfortable with the notion of self-praise, and feel awkward when it comes to celebrating our good qualities.

Self-compassion teaches us that in order to become truly happy and fulfilled, we must recognize the whole picture. We need and deserve acknowledgement for our positive attributes and accomplishments, along with compassion for our areas of weakness. Just as we freely offer praise to those around us, we too deserve this same measure of recognition for our strengths and achievements. This next exercise, drawn from the work of Kristin Neff (2011), starts us down this path of self-appreciation.

Instructions: In the space below, list five things about yourself that you appreciate and feel good about. Remember that if discomfort arises, the aim of this is not to claim that you're perfect or even better than anyone else; rather, it's to merely appreciate the things that you like about yourself. Take your time, and begin by writing down **five aspects about yourself that you are proud of, and can appreciate.**

1. _____
2. _____
3. _____
4. _____
5. _____

Once you've completed your list, choose <u>one</u> of the positive aspects you came up with to focus on a bit more. Close your eyes, and allow yourself to take a moment and reflect on this good trait or characteristic. Recognize that this good thing is part of who you are and allow yourself to feel and enjoy the positive feelings that arise from this recognition. Take a moment to savor these feelings, letting them linger for a moment before opening your eyes.

Self-Compassion Practice #5: Self-Criticism Versus Self-Compassion

We've discussed in this chapter some of the many reasons we engage in self-criticism. Oftentimes, we hold a deep-rooted belief that self-criticism will somehow motivate us, spurring us to greater heights. Yet all too often the opposite holds true. Self-criticism demoralizes us, and discourages us from our pursuits. In this exercise, you'll explore the ways in which **self-criticism can undercut our goals, and how self-compassion can be the antidote to this tendency.**

Instructions: Reflect on a personal trait that you tend to be self-critical around, or a particular habit for which you try to motivate yourself through self-criticism. What goals do you attempt to reach by using self-criticism as a source of motivation? How well does this tend to work, and how do you tend to feel in those moments? Try to think about a specific, perhaps ongoing, battle in which you find yourself struggling. **What might it be like to use a kinder, gentler way of relating to yourself in these moments?** How would a kind, compassionate friend or loved one speak towards you? Feel free to use the following prompting questions to help get you started:

- Habit/trait that I struggle with: _____
  _____

- Self-critical language that I use (be specific): _____
  _____

- How this makes me feel: _____
  _____

- Self-compassionate alternative (be specific): _____
  _____

- How this makes me feel: _____
  _____

- Behavioral outcome: _____
  _____

(Continued)

On a personal level, I struggled for years to consistently maintain an ongoing exercise regimen. I would go through stretches of regularly running or working out at the gym, only to fall back into old habits. For many years, I would attempt to motivate myself through negative self-talk, believing that self-criticism would jumpstart me back on track. For short periods of time this would work, but over time the constant verbal beatings had the opposite effect. It took a toll on my self-esteem, and made me even less likely to take care of my body.

It wasn't until I discovered the notion of self-compassion that this began to turn around. I'm still far from perfect, but nowadays I can treat myself with kindness and love, which (contrary to my initial assumptions) has actually made me <u>more</u> able to maintain a regular exercise habit. Over the next few weeks, notice when you catch yourself using self-criticism as a motivator. Notice how it makes you feel and whether it seems to take you further from your goals. Try speaking to yourself in a kinder, more supportive manner. The results may surprise you.

The Path of Optimism

"There is nothing either good or bad, but thinking makes it so."
—William Shakespeare (Hamlet, Act 2)

THE TWO TRAVELERS

An ancient Zen tale tells the story of two travelers who stumbled across a farmer while passing through the mountains. The first traveler was weary, and stopped for a brief rest by the side of the road. "I'm on my way to the next town," he said turning to the farmer, "can you tell me what the people there are like?" The farmer looked up, and responded to the traveler with a question of his own. "What were the people like in the last town you passed through?" he asked.

The traveler responded by bemoaning his experiences in the last town. "It was awful," he lamented. "No one spoke my language, it was cold, and they made me sleep on the floor. Not only that, they fed me a strange dish that tasted just terrible. I hope I never have to go back to that town," the traveler remarked. The farmer paused, stroking his chin, and replied, "Well sadly, I think that you'll find the people in the next town to be no different." And so the first traveler solemnly resumed his journey.

Several hours passed, and another traveler passed through. Like the first, this one was weary and stopped briefly to catch his breath and regroup. Turning to the farmer, the traveler stated, "I'm on my way to the next town. Can you tell me what the people there are like?" The farmer looked up from his fieldwork, and again responded to the question with a question of his own. "What were the people like in the last town you passed through?" he asked.

The traveler could barely contain his excitement. "They were wonderful!" he burst out. "They treated me so kindly, even though nobody spoke my language. They fed me their traditional food, which was different from anything I've ever tasted before. And though it was cold and I had to sleep on the ground, they gave me blankets and tried their best to help me stay warm. I enjoyed my time there so much, I didn't want to leave," the traveler exclaimed.

Pausing again while stroking his chin, the farmer turned to the traveler and said, "You're in luck, because I think you'll find that the people in the next town will be no different." The second traveler went happily on his way, excited about the adventures yet to come.

****

At its core, the tale of the two travelers underscores one of the key factors influencing our happiness. Whereas the first traveler illustrates the cost of a pessimistic mindset, the second traveler exemplifies one of the seven paths to happiness: the path of optimism. The lens through which we view our world may not seem like such a big deal, but countless studies now demonstrate the immense benefits of optimism, as well as the tremendous consequences of pessimism.

We are often told to "look on the bright side," or to learn how to "see the glass as half full." While these recommendations may seem trite or even silly, they nonetheless hold great truth. There have now been countless studies showing both the negative consequences of pessimism, as well as the profound benefits of optimism (Seligman, 2006). Optimists perform better across nearly all areas of life, including mental health, physical health, and relationships. They tend to do better in school, perform better at work, and even live substantially longer lives on average.

In short, it pays to be an optimist. But as with any skill, becoming more optimistic is easier said than done. For many, the tendency to see the world through a filter of pessimism may feel so deeply engrained that change seems like a hopeless cause. But if you consider yourself to be somewhat of a pessimist, there's good news. Countless studies and interventions now demonstrate that changing our mindset and increasing our level of optimism is indeed possible.

At the end of the chapter I will introduce a series of practical skills you can begin incorporating into your life in order to lastingly increase your level of optimism. Thankfully, becoming an optimist doesn't require good genes or good luck; rather, it is a skill that we can all learn and practice, in order to harness its immense benefits.

WHAT IS OPTIMISM?

As with many ideas presented in this book, the concept of optimism may mean different things to different people and requires a bit of unpacking. The word optimism itself is drawn from the Latin word *optimum*, which translates roughly to mean "best." Therefore, at its core, optimism is closely connected to seeing things in a good light, both in regards to our future as well as events that occur within our lives. Drawing from the latest research in the field, and for the purposes of this book, we will consider optimism as compriseing two separate but interconnected components: our view towards the future, and the manner in which we make sense of things that happen in our lives.

The first component of optimism, referred to by psychologists as *dispositional optimism*, consists of the manner in which we look towards the future. Do we look forward with excited anticipation, expecting that things will turn out well in our life? Or do we nervously glance ahead with worry, believing that storm clouds are approaching? In general, optimism about the future refers to the belief that the days to come will be mostly positive, that we will accomplish our goals and achieve our hopes, and that the future holds promise. This aspect of optimism is most closely connected to the ideas of seeing the glass as half full, looking on the bright side, or finding the silver lining in a cloud.

The second aspect of optimism has to do with the concept of our *explanatory style,* and is referred to as *attributional optimism*. According to Martin Seligman, explanatory style refers to the "manner in which you habitually explain to yourself why events happen" (Seligman, 2006). From this standpoint, when we experience a setback in our life, we have a choice as far as how we interpret what happened. We can choose to look at things in a charitable, optimistic manner. Or we can interpret what just occurred in a more negative light.

As Seligman explains, there are three dimensions to our explanatory style: *permanence, pervasiveness,* and *personalization* (Seligman, 2006). Optimists and pessimists display opposite patterns in terms of these dimensions when explaining things that happen in their lives. When faced with a setback, optimists tend to think of the situation as being *temporary, specific,* and *external.* Conversely, pessimists consider setbacks to be *permanent, universal,* and *internal.* By comparison, when things go well, optimists tend to think it's due to permanent, universal, and internal factors, while pessimists believe that their success is due to temporary, specific, and external factors.

What does this look like in real life? Let's say you perform well on your chemistry midterm exam. An optimist would attribute this to factors that are more internal, long lasting, and stable. If you're an optimist, you'll likely say things to yourself like "I'm good at chemistry," or "I'm a good test taker." If you're pessimist, by contrast, you'll tend to look at this success as being merely temporary, fleeting, and external. Beliefs like, "I got lucky," or "the teacher gave an easy exam," might be running through your mind.

Conversely, let's say you bombed that midterm exam. Well, if you're an optimist you'll probably take it in stride and attribute your performance to external, temporary, and specific factors. You might say, "I didn't study enough for the test, and I got a bit unlucky, but I'll do better the next time." If you're a pessimist though, you'll make judgments about yourself that are much harsher. "I'm such a failure" or "I'll never pass this class."

Equally important to understanding what optimism is however, is recognizing what optimism is *not*. The classic children's book *Pollyanna* tells the story of a young orphan whose philosophy of life consists of finding the good in any situation, no matter how dire. Even when faced with losing the use of her legs, Pollyanna manages to bounce back and remain cheerful and sunny. While it would perhaps be nice to have such unbridled hopefulness, the goal of optimism training is not to help you channel your inner-Pollyanna. Nor is it to come to believe that life will be free from setbacks, troubles, or pain. Rather, our aim is to gain a more positive view of our future, while learning to view our setbacks or troubles in a *realistic* but positive manner.

Taken together, we can see that the path of optimism entails both looking at our future in positive terms, and learning to interpret both the good and the bad in our life in a more adaptive manner. Both components of optimism are crucial, and in the pages to come you will be introduced to a series of skills designed to help boost both your *dispositional* and *attributional* optimism. But if being an optimist is so important for happiness, why then is it often so hard to do?

THE COST OF PESSIMISM

As we discussed in the second chapter, one of our main foes when it comes to boosting our happiness comes from an unlikely source – our brain. To recap, our brains were developed over millennia with a singular purpose in mind: the survival of our species. They were not, and are not, built with happiness as the ultimate goal. This doesn't at all mean that happiness is unachievable, for it surely is. But in order to survive, our brains developed in order to anticipate threats, attend to danger, and live to see another day. Viewed in this light, pessimism is a natural byproduct of a brain finely tuned to focus on the negative at the expense of the positive.

Although pessimism makes sense from an evolutionary perspective, it comes at a great cost when it comes to personal happiness and well-being. There is no substantial evidence that pessimists perform worse than optimists across a wide range of areas (Seligman, 2006; Lyubomirsky, 2008). They exhibit worse outcomes in terms of mental health and relationship satisfaction. Their health suffers, with rates of many illnesses higher among pessimists, and they may even have shorter lifespans. When faced with challenges, pessimists tend to give up rather than persevere, compared to optimists who are more likely to push through obstacles.

For many of us, a pessimistic disposition may feel deeply engrained and intractable. And to be sure, there is certainly evidence that factors such as genes and inborn temperament play a role in whether we are more of a "glass half full" versus "glass half empty" kind of person. But even if you consider yourself to be on the pessimistic end of the spectrum, there's good news. Findings suggest that in many cases, optimism can be learned, and is a skill no different from any other.

OPTIMISM: GOOD FOR OUR MINDS

The notion that how we think dictates how we feel is not a new one. Indeed, centuries ago the Greek philosopher Epictetus noted that, "Men are disturbed not by things, but by what we make of them." In *Paradise Lost*, Milton writes, heaven." And the Buddha observed that, "Our life is a creation of our mind." Each of these sentiments shares the idea that our mindset holds great power when it comes to our emotional experience.

Modern psychological research supports these ancient truths. The burgeoning field of cognitive therapy, for example, emphasizes the link between how we think and how we feel. Founded by psychologists Aaron Beck and Albert Ellis, and revolutionized further by pioneers such as David Burns, cognitive therapy demonstrates the immense power of one's thoughts and beliefs on his or her emotional experience. In other words, when we harshly judge ourselves, ruminate on past failures, or anticipate that negative things will happen to us, we'll feel lousy. If, on the other hand, we learn to think in a more realistic, positive, and adaptive manner, we'll feel much better. Either way, our mindset determines much of our emotional experiences.

At its core, pessimism is closely connected with a host of mental health problems, including depression and anxiety. Individuals with depression, almost by definition, experience negative expectations about their future and feel helpless to change them. In this light, we can see how the two aspects of optimism that we discussed earlier play a crucial role in the development or prevention of depression. Conversely, anxiety has been described as a "future-oriented mood state," in which we attempt to cope with negative events that have not yet occurred. This again, on a theoretical level, can be thought of as the direct opposite of an optimistic point of view.

The theoretical link between optimism, pessimism, and mental health has now been supported in numerous studies. Optimists perform better than pessimists on a range of mental health measures, most notably a significantly lower rate of depression (Hart, 2008; Chang, 2001). Optimism has also been shown to be a strong protective factor against suicide, whereas pessimism and hopelessness is considered a strong risk factor (Hirsch, 2007). Furthermore, optimists tend to suffer from lower rates of anxiety and stress compared to pessimists (Seligman, 2006), and report higher levels of overall life satisfaction and happiness (Lyubomirsky, 2007).

On a brain-based level, further differences emerge between optimists and pessimists. According to Elaine Fox, a neuroscientist based in the United Kingdom, optimists tend to display greater activation on the left side of their brain, whereas pessimists show increased activation on the right side (Fox, 2013). As you'll recall, left-sided brain activity is more connected to positive emotions, whereas right-sided activation tends to be associated with negative emotional states. Fortunately, the principle of neuroplasticity supports the notion that through practice and intentional activity, these brain patterns can be changed over time. So even if you're a dyed-in-the-wool pessimist, your brain can in fact be "rewired" for optimism.

These mental health benefits of optimism are indeed substantial, and for many of us they provide sufficient motivation to start changing our mindset. But as it turns out, the emotional perks of optimism are only part of the picture.

OPTIMISM: GOOD FOR OUR BODIES

Many people have long assumed that our health is a purely physical matter, determined by factors such as our genes, diet, and dumb luck. But exciting findings in recent years suggest that our mind plays a crucial role in impacting our physical health. As with many of the other paths to happiness discussed in this book, optimism too plays an important part in determining our physical health. There have now been numerous studies on the impact of optimism on health, and nearly all support the same finding: that optimists tend to perform consistently better than pessimists across a range of health indicators. In his book entitled *Learned Optimism*, Professor Martin Seligman reviews many of these findings, and outlines the myriad advantages optimism holds in terms of health. Among other things, optimists appear to have better overall physical health, and even tend to catch fewer colds than pessimists. Their immune systems tend to function better, enabling them to bounce back from illness more quickly and efficiently.

Further studies underscore the perks of being an optimist when it comes to our health. In one notable study conducted through the Harvard School of Public Health, scientists examined the role of positive emotions on cardiovascular health (Boehm & Kubzansky, 2012). The researchers found a strong correlation between positive psychological well-being and improved heart health. But of all the factors they examined, optimism appeared to have the biggest impact on cardiovascular functioning. Regardless of other influences such as socioeconomic status, age, or body weight, optimism was found to drastically reduce the risk of heart attacks and strokes. Among the most optimistic participants, their risk of a major cardiovascular event was reduced by as much as *50 percent*!

As if the findings above weren't enough, it appears that an optimistic attitude can also help in another key area: our lifespan. The search for longevity leads people down a multitude of roads, including exercise, vitamins, health foods, and more. But recent research suggests that optimism may provide us with the ultimate "fountain of youth." Of the many factors that have been studied, optimism may in fact be among the most powerful. For example, in a longevity study conducted in the Netherlands, researchers found that participants who felt that they still have something to strive for and look forward to were found to live significantly longer lives (Giltay, 2004, 2006).

Another study conducted at the University of Pittsburgh found similar results, and even discovered that optimists were less likely to die from a host of diseases such as cancer, diabetes, and heart disease (Tindle, 2009). To many, these findings may seem too good to be true, or even farfetched. And indeed, most of us prefer to grasp onto the tangible when it comes to our health. But much like stopping smoking or improving our diet, cultivating an optimistic attitude has been shown to have a powerful effect on our bodies and our physical health.

OPTIMISM: GOOD FOR OUR LIVES

As shown above, an optimistic mindset can lead to vastly improved mental and physical health. But the benefits don't stop there. Indeed, whether one looks at performance in the workplace, at the ballot box, or on the playing field, an optimistic mindset has been shown to be a powerful predictor of success.

Many sports fans have long held the notion that the mental aspect of performance can be just as crucial as the physical. As Yogi Berra once put it as only he could, "Ninety percent of this game is half mental." But does this notion turn out to be true? And can optimism explain the success of athletes above and beyond other factors? As it happens, multiple studies have looked at this very question, with some astounding results. In an early look at the link between athletic performance and optimism, researchers pored over newspaper clippings of several teams from the National Basketball Association along with major league baseball. They then coded various quotes from the players, coaches, and managers according to how optimistic or pessimistic they appeared and then compared these ratings to the actual performance of the teams.

Upon analyzing the data, the researchers discovered that optimism was strongly linked with improved performance on the field (Seligman, 2006). Not only that, it actually appeared to *predict* future success for these teams, meaning that it wasn't simply a case of players exhibiting optimism *because* they were already successful. Rather, they achieved success *because* they were optimistic. Later studies built on these findings, and found that optimism was closely linked to the success of athletes across a range of sports, including Olympic swimmers and professional football players. Beyond the playing field, similar methods were used to show that optimism is even strongly connected to determining which candidates we back for president. Indeed, findings suggest that the relative degree of optimism or pessimism displayed by presidential candidates is a strong predictor of who will end up winning the contest.

Although these findings are fascinating, they have limited implications for most of us. After all, few readers will end up being elected president or playing in the NBA. So it certainly begs the question, what can optimism do for the rest of us? Quite a bit, according to the latest research. Studies persuasively show that an optimistic mindset is strongly associated with better performance at school and at work. Not only that, it appears to help our bank accounts as well.

As an example, one study conducted at Duke University looked at optimistic and pessimistic attitudes among business school students. The researchers found that optimistic graduates were far more likely to find jobs following graduation than those students who tended more towards pessimism (Kaniel & Robinson, 2011). And among those who did obtain jobs, the optimists earned more money on average, and were more likely to be promoted and advance in their companies. So if you want to succeed in the workplace, it pays to be an optimist.

How and Why is Optimism so Helpful?

Having an optimistic mindset, coupled with utilizing an optimistic explanatory style, has been shown to have a powerful effect on our mind, our bodies, and our lives. As described in the preceding pages of this chapter, optimists perform better than pessimists across a host of domains, including mental health, physical health, work performance, and interpersonal relationships. Best of all, optimism is a skill like any other and can be learned and cultivated to help transform our lives. But why is optimism such a powerful tool in our quest for happiness? Why does it have such an impact on our well-being? The answers lie in a few areas, which we'll now turn our attention to:

- *Optimism helps us cope with challenges.* When faced with challenges and stressors, individuals with a pessimistic mindset and style will often give up. Optimists, by contrast, are better able to persevere and cope with challenging circumstances (Segerstrom, 2001). Even during times of severe duress, studies show that optimists are better able to maintain a positive outlook and utilize healthier strategies for coping (Scheier & Carver, 2010).

- *Optimism helps us achieve goals.* Because optimists are by definition oriented to a positive future, they are more likely to set and reach goals in their lives.

- *Optimism breeds positive emotions.* When we engage in strategies of optimism, this can often lead to a cascade of other positive emotional states, resulting in an "upward spiral" of well-being (Frederickson, 2009).

- *Optimism increases social support.* A frequent finding in the literature suggests that optimists are far more likely than pessimists to both receive and utilize social support. As we'll learn more about in a later chapter, social connection is a powerful force in our lives, and is crucial for well-being. It turns out that optimists tend to have stronger social networks, providing yet another reason to foster an optimistic mindset.

- *Optimism short-circuits rumination.* Rumination refers to our tendency to focus our attention on the sources and consequences of our distress, rather than engage in solution-focused problem-solving. It is a powerful predictor of both depression and anxiety, with depression being marked by rumination about the past, whereas anxiety is more associated with rumination about the future. As it happens, optimism is a powerful antidote for rumination, as it helps us engage in goal-setting and problem-solving in the face of stress.

- *Optimism changes our brain.* As described earlier in the chapter, an optimistic mindset has been shown to lead to changes on even a brain-based level. These neuronal changes may account for some of the many benefits offered by optimism.

- *Optimism buffers us from mental health problems.* Perhaps due to its effect on rumination, optimism has been found to be a strong protective factor against a host of mental health difficulties.

Tips for Boosting Optimism

In the next section, we'll begin practicing a series of scientifically proven strategies designed to help boost your level of optimism in a lasting way. But first, we'll review a handful of guidelines and tips that can help you in your journey. Bear in mind of course that these are just guidelines, so feel free to experiment a bit with what works best for you.

Don't try to be Pollyanna. Optimism works best when it is fostered in a *realistic* manner. Remember, the goal isn't to trick ourselves into believing that everything is perfect in our lives, and that we will be free from pain and worry forever. Rather, we want to strive for an accurate and credible sort of optimism, one that Martin Seligman refers to as "flexible optimism."

Remember the past. Oftentimes, our best sources for optimism come from obstacles we've already overcome. So when we're stuck feeling hopeless, or unable to cope with what life has thrown at us, we can almost always look back on obstacles we've managed to conquer in the past. Remembering these can give us the strength and courage to face what's in front of us.

Track positive experiences. If you tend to gravitate towards pessimism or negativity, experiment with trying to notice the more positive and hopeful experiences you encounter throughout your day. A powerful strategy might include utilizing the "Three Good

Things" exercise introduced in Chapter 4, which can help shift our outlook more towards optimism.

Surround yourself with positivity. It's easy to forget sometimes how strong of an influence the people around us have on our mood and happiness. If you're someone who tends to surround yourself with people who tend towards pessimism, try experimenting a bit with the people whom you associate with and how this impacts you. You might be surprised at how much of a difference it can make to spend more time around optimists!

Be mindful of your language. Our own self-talk contains powerful clues regarding our level of optimism or pessimism. By becoming more aware of the language we use in this regard, we can begin the process towards change. Next time you find yourself feeling frustrated or wanting to give up on something, try noticing the way you're talking to yourself in that very moment. Be especially on the lookout for negative remarks such as "I'll never get this right," or "I can't do this."

Make it a habit. As with all the strategies outlined in this book, optimism is a learned skill that we can all improve on if we're willing to put in the work. But like any new practice, it's important to turn it into a habit in order to fully make a change in our lives. So whichever strategy you gravitate to in the next session, it's crucial to find ways to turn it into an ongoing practice in the days to come.

OPTIMISM PRACTICES

Optimism Practice #1: Slow and Steady Wins the Race

Earlier this year, I had the opportunity to go on a trek in the Peruvian Andes on the way up to visit Machu Picchu. It was truly a once in a lifetime experience, filled with indescribable beauty and incredible culture. But I must admit I was not quite up to the challenge physically at times. Our group trekked great distances at high altitudes each day, and I was stricken by altitude sickness midway through the trip. At several points I even thought of quitting, feeling that my body couldn't last the entire journey.

It was at this point that I noticed how our guide traversed the land with grace and ease, effortlessly chugging along on the way up the mountain. I asked him what his secret was, half-jokingly and not expecting much of a response. "Just one foot in front of the other," he said back to me. "I don't look at the top of the mountain, and how far away it seems. I just think about the next step I have to take."

When our guide said that to me, I was reminded of a piece of ancient wisdom from the Chinese philosopher Lao Tzu, who reminds us that the **"journey of a thousand miles begins with a single step."** Armed with this reminder, I stopped thinking about how on earth I would be able to finish the entire trek and reach the summit. Instead, I began thinking about how I would make it through the next step, the next quarter mile, the next mile, and so forth. I became more immersed in the present moment, and was even more able to experience and appreciate the beauty that surrounded me. Before I knew it, I was standing at the top of the pass, out of breath and exhausted, but happy.

Pessimism often stems from feeling that we cannot possibly reach the finish line from where we are standing. We look off in the distance and the ground in between where we are and where we wish to go feels insurmountable. But just as we cannot scale an entire ladder in one single step, we must remember that the path to reaching our goals is a longer journey. **In this optimism-building exercise, we'll be thinking about goals that you have for the future, and breaking them up into more manageable sub-goals.** Whereas large-scale goals can sometimes feel overwhelming and unachievable, the steps in between are eminently doable. By focusing on these instead, we can shift from pessimism to optimism.

(Continued)

Instructions: Take a moment and reflect on some of the goals and dreams you have for the future. Consider different domains of your life, including your career, relationship, friendships, and family. Although reflecting on these hopes can feel inspiring and exciting at times, it can also feel overwhelming when we think of tackling it all at once. Pessimism can often set in, making us feel less able to achieve out goals. To overcome this obstacle, it can be helpful to break down our larger goals and dreams into shorter-term sub-goals that can be completed a step at a time. You can use any format that works for you, but if it helps, feel free to use the following prompts to get you started:

Long-Term Goal:

_____

_____

_____

When I hope to achieve this by:_____

What is the <u>first</u> step I need to take in order to achieve this?

_____

_____

_____

Who can I turn to for help in reaching my goal?

_____

_____

_____

What do I need to accomplish within 1 month?

_____

_____

_____

What do I need to accomplish within 3-6 months?

_____

_____

_____

Optimism Practice #2: Overcoming Pessimism

We all engage in negative thinking from time to time. But negative, pessimistic self-talk can carry a great cost. It can demoralize us, lower our mood, and make us less likely to achieve our goals. Worse yet, pessimistic thinking can create a downward spiral, whereby negative thoughts create negative moods, which in turn spawns further pessimism. Oftentimes these sorts of thoughts fly under the radar, barely perceptible in our conscious awareness. But through mindfulness and greater self-awareness, we can learn about these patterns and stop them in their tracks.

In this next optimism-building exercise, you'll first be learning to identify the negative or pessimistic thoughts that get in your way, and then learning to replace them with a more realistic way of thinking. As the Greek philosopher Epictetus reminds us, we are "disturbed not by things, but by what we make of them." Therefore our thoughts, or interpretations, of what happens in our lives are crucial. By slowly learning to shift our thinking away from negativity and pessimism, we can change the way we feel by changing the way we think. Remember, the goal isn't to channel our inner "Pollyanna," or to develop an unrealistically positive outlook. Rather, realism and truth is the name of the game.

__Instructions:__ For the next week, notice and write down negative or pessimistic thoughts that get in the way of your happiness. Monitor your inner self-talk for clues about the sorts of thoughts that seem to be most problematic for you. For example, when you feel frustrated or discouraged, you might notice thoughts such as "I'll never be able to finish this project," or "I'm such a failure, I'll never get that promotion at work." Whenever you feel bad in a given moment, bring your awareness to the way in which you are internally "talking" to yourself. Once you've noticed a few of these negative thoughts or beliefs that you struggle with, write them down here:

Negative Thought #1:_____

_____

Negative Thought #2:_____

_____

Negative Thought #3:_____

_____

(Continued)

Next, begin the process of challenging these thoughts. See if you can reinterpret the situation in a more realistic manner, and over time begin to replace your negative, pessimistic thoughts with a more balanced perspective. Depending on the nature of your negative thoughts, some questions to consider when challenging them might include:

- Is this thought a fact, or is it merely a thought?

  _____

- What would I say to a close friend or loved one in this situation?

  _____

  _____

- What might a close friend or loved one say to me?

  _____

  _____

- Is there another way to look at this situation?

  _____

  _____

- Are there any factors I might be missing here?

  _____

  _____

- Is this situation truly as important in the grand scheme of things as it feels?

  _____

  _____

- Am I overgeneralizing at all, or missing the bigger picture?

  _____

- What would a more balanced way of looking at this be?

  _____

  _____

Picture yourself as a good trial lawyer or cross-examiner, poking holes in your negative or pessimistic thoughts as they arise. As a reminder, the goal is not merely to "think positive." Rather, the path to overcoming negativity lies in learning to see things in a realistic and balanced manner.

Optimism Practice #3: A Positive Future

This next optimism-boosting strategy is drawn from the work of psychologist Laura King, who developed one of the first studies designed to scientifically boost optimistic thinking. In her study, King asked people to visit her laboratory for 4 consecutive days, and to engage in a writing exercise aimed to tap into optimism and increase it over time. Specifically, King asked her volunteers to spend twenty minutes writing in a journal about their "best possible future self" over the course of the four days they were in the study (King, 2001). Participants were instructed to imagine what their life might look like in the future if all their dreams came true and hopes were realized.

Although it might not seem that a brief writing exercise like this would make much of a change, the results were nothing short of remarkable. Compared to those in the control group (who were asked to write about other unrelated topics), those who wrote about their "best possible future self" were found to be **significantly happier for weeks** following their completion of the exercise. Not only that, they had **better physical health outcomes, and were less likely to fall ill**, for several months following the study.

Why did King's exercise lead to such powerful changes? It appears that not only did the exercise feel good in the moment, it also helped participants feel empowered to make positive changes in their lives moving forward. In other words, by focusing on and writing about their best possible future, **participants in the study were actually more able to make positive and meaningful changes in their lives starting immediately.** Writing about this positive future may have also helped them tap into what they most valued and wanted in their lives, and inspired them to set goals to begin achieving those desired outcomes. With these benefits in mind, let's start practicing.

Instructions: For the next week, set aside twenty minutes per day to journal about your positive future. Picture yourself five or ten years from now, and imagine that things in your life have gone as well as you could have hoped for. Your dreams have been realized, and you have achieved your deepest and most meaningful goals. Close your eyes, and spend a few moments conjuring this image. Consider different domains of your life, including your relationships, career, family, and hobbies. Allow yourself to bask in this vivid image, and to savor the feelings that come up as you do. When you are ready, begin writing about what you imagined on a separate piece of paper.

Optimism Practice #4:
Explain Setbacks Like an Optimist

Earlier in this chapter, we discussed Martin Seligman's notion of *explanatory style*, which refers to the manner in which we explain events in our lives. For example, when we face a setback, our explanatory style can either be optimistic ("I got unlucky that time, and things will work out better next time"), or it can be pessimistic ("I'm a failure, and things never go my way").

According to Seligman, optimists and pessimists display opposite patterns when it comes to explaining negative events that occur in their lives. When faced with adversity, optimists tend to think of the situation as being *temporary*, *specific*, and *external*. Conversely, pessimists display a tendency to attribute setbacks to *permanent*, *universal*, and *internal* factors. What does this look like in real life? Let's pretend for a moment that you recently got passed over for an important promotion at work. An optimist might respond by saying, "I didn't prep enough for that interview," or "I'll surely get it the next time." A pessimist, by contrast, might respond by saying, "I'm such a loser," or "I'll never get ahead in life."

In this final optimism practice, notice the way in which you talk to yourself when faced with setbacks or adversity. For the next week, keep track of moments when things don't go your way, and notice the way you respond internally to these situations. If your tendency is to view these sorts of setbacks in a pessimistic manner, see if you can gently shift your viewpoint to a more optimistic viewpoint. Over time, this internal practice will become more habitual, helping you to view adversity through the prism of optimism rather than pessimism.

Optimism Practice #5: Reflecting on Success

One of the best ways to remind ourselves that things will turn out OK in life is to **reflect on times when we've already overcome hardship or adversity.** To increase optimism, therefore, we needn't look any further than our own history of successes and triumphs. By reminding ourselves of these experiences, we can nip pessimism in the bud and remain on track.

Unfortunately, in moments of pessimism, it can be hard to remember many of these previous successes. Part of this is due to the fact that our memory can be *mood-dependent*, meaning that it's harder to recall instances of accomplishment during times of pessimism or hopelessness. Therefore, this exercise is best completed when you are in a positive state of mind. You can then look back on your answers when your mood sinks, helping to pull you out of this funk.

Instructions: Think back on a time from the past in which you've been successful at achieving an important goal. Take a moment and think back on various accomplishments you have reached in various domains in your life. Consider successes at school, at work, and in your relationships. **On a separate sheet of paper, choose one of these triumphs and write about the success in greater detail.** If you find it helpful, feel free to repeat this with various other successes you've had in your life. To help you get started, consider the following questions:

- What was the nature of your success?
  _____

- How hard did you work to attain it?
  _____

- Were there times when you thought of giving up?
  If so, what kept you going?
  _____

- Who did you receive support from during the process?
  _____

- What did you learn from reaching this goal?
  _____

- How does it feel to reflect on this success?
  _____

Chapter 10

The Path of Connection

"Happiness is Love. Full Stop."

–George Vaillant

REAL LIFE CONNECTION

For over forty years, George Vaillant patiently served as the director of a long-running research project at Harvard University. One of the world's preeminent psychiatrists, Vaillant had spent his career researching a wide range of important topics in the field of mental health, including schizophrenia, addiction, defense mechanisms, and personality development. But the aims of this particular study were a bit different, and not exactly modest in nature. Its goal: To discover what leads to human flourishing.

It all began in the late 1930's, before the United States had even entered the Second World War. Over the course of a few years, a group of male college sophomores were recruited to be part of a study aimed at determining which sorts of factors led to health rather than illness. William Grant, one of the earliest funders of the study, was a well-known department store mogul at the time. Grant hoped to learn more about what sorts of individuals would make successful managers, to help make his business even more prosperous. Though the original founders of the study had high hopes, even they could not have envisioned how important the "Grant Study of Human Development" would someday become.

The 268 sophomores who were recruited into the study were perhaps not your average college students. The subject pool included four future senators, a future member of the President's Cabinet, and even a United States president (John F. Kennedy, in case you were curious). The study was designed to be *longitudinal*, meaning that the researchers hoped to track these individuals for many years in order to view their development over time. Originally, the researchers figured that twenty or twenty-five years would suffice, but they ended up tracking the men for much longer. Indeed, the study ended up lasting over seventy years!

Years later, armed with decades of data about what had become of the 268 men in the study, Vaillant began poring over the findings. He examined all sorts of factors, and measured their impact on the men's lives. Some of the participants had of course dropped away over the years, but a remarkably high number of them remained connected to the study and were able to provide powerful clues about the nature of well-being, happiness, and successful aging. Vaillant studied dozens of factors, including income, marital satisfaction, physical health, political affiliation, and substance use habits.

Some of the initial findings of the study were not surprising. For example, alcohol abuse was found to be one of the most destructive influences on marriage, health, and overall happiness levels among the participants. Yet of all the factors Vaillant analyzed, he was most surprised by the immense power that social connection had on the lives of the men in his study. Vaillant found that having warm social connections was strongly associated with improved mental and physical health, greater job success, and a host of other benefits.

"The only thing that really matters in life are your relationships to other people," Vaillant once famously stated. One of the world's most accomplished and gifted researchers, Vaillant was once asked to sum up what he had learned about the nature of happiness and well-being. He replied: "The seventy-five years and twenty million dollars expended on the Grant Study points to a straightforward five-word conclusion: Happiness is love. Full stop."

****

One of the most consistent and robust findings in the field of mental health is that happier people tend to have stronger connections with friends, family, spouses, and co-workers. It's not merely a case that happier people tend to have better relationships because they're happy to begin with. Rather, there is clearly a bidirectional relationship between social connection and happiness, whereby increased social support leads to increased happiness, which in turn makes us more able to seek out further social support around us.

In this chapter, we'll first discuss the importance of social connection in our lives, and discuss what sort of connection truly matters in terms of our well-being. We'll then turn our attention to a series of practices designed to help you achieve greater closeness and intimacy in your life. By doing so, you'll be well on your way to becoming a happier, not to mention healthier person.

THE IMPORTANCE OF CONNECTION

Imagine for a moment that you're at your doctor's office for your annual health screening and checkup. She gauges your vital signs, measuring your heart rate and blood pressure. You step on the scale in order to be weighed, and breathe in and out slowly as she listens to your heartbeat through her stethoscope. Your doctor scrutinizes your latest lab levels, perhaps checking your glucose and cholesterol readings. She then proceeds to ask you a series of health-related questions about your habits and behaviors. How much have you been drinking alcohol or smoking cigarettes? How frequently have you been exercising, and how rigorously? What sort of diet have you been eating?

When our doctor asks us these sorts of questions, we usually don't bat an eye. After all, we've come to expect these sorts of queries when it comes to our health. And we recognize that habits like substance use, smoking, exercise, and diet all play an important role in helping us maintain good health. But imagine for a moment that she begins asking you a different series of questions altogether. What are your friendships like? Do you have someone you can confide in when you're feeling stressed? How close are you with your spouse? Do you feel close with your support network?

Hearing these sorts of questions at a health checkup might seem strange at first, but perhaps it shouldn't. After all, if she were interested in assessing your overall health, your doctor would be wise to ask about your social connections. Studies now show that the nature and quality of our interpersonal connections is one of the most powerful predictors of both mental and physical health. Individuals with strong social support have been shown to be healthier overall, with lower rates of illness and increased longevity. They have better mental health outcomes, with lower rates of depression along with greater happiness levels. They perform better at work, and even earn higher salaries.

BORN TO CONNECT

Human beings are profoundly social creatures, and we are strongly influenced by what happens around us in our social world. For example, if you live with a roommate who's depressed, you're significantly more likely to become depressed yourself. If someone you know were to quit smoking cigarettes, you'd be far more likely to quit as well. And if the person next to you in the cafeteria decides to eat a salad, you're far more likely to order something healthy too. These and other fascinating findings are outlined in an exciting book entitled *Connected* by Nicholas Christakis and James Fowler, professors at Harvard University and UC San Diego, respectively. *Connected* describes the interconnected nature of our lives, and the importance of social bonds in our day-to-day life. Why is social connection so deeply rooted in our very being? Some answers lie distant in the past.

The human brain developed over time for survival, and part of survival entailed having to form and sustain social bonds. Relative to other animals, we humans have disproportionately large brains. This puzzled scientists for some time, but in recent decades some theories have emerged that might help explain this phenomenon. Dubbed the "social brain hypothesis," researchers have now mapped out a direct correlation between brain size and group size in the animal kingdom (Dunbar, 2003). In other words, the more social interaction an animal must navigate, the larger its brain must be. Human beings, with the most complex and layered social networks of any species on earth, had to develop significantly larger brains in order to survive and thrive.

As our species developed and evolved, social grouping became imperative for survival. Indeed, the ability to create and maintain social bonds was as important to early man as the ability to throw a stone or build a fire. Social groups enabled early humans to stave off starvation, to hunt together, and to fight off enemies together. Social bonds empowered humans to reproduce, protect their children, and raise them in safety and security.

From an evolutionary standpoint, the importance of social connection therefore makes good sense. But modern neuroscience has shed even further light on the ways in which our brains are wired to be social. Matthew Lieberman, a neuroscientist at UCLA, has persuasively argued that our brains have developed over the millennia to seek out and value social connection and interpersonal bonds. In his recent book entitled *Social: Why Our Brains Are Wired to Connect*, Lieberman outlines how our brains contain a series of neural networks designed to foster social connection with those around us. Summing up his years of research on cognitive neuroscience, Lieberman stated that, "this is what our brains were wired for: reaching out to and interacting with others. These social adaptations are central to making us the most successful species on earth." But if connection is so important, and such a deeply ingrained aspect of our species, why is connection often so hard to come by?

QUALITY CONNECTIONS

In his thought-provoking book entitled *Bowling Alone*, sociologist Robert Putnam eloquently illustrates how Americans have become less connected to one another over the past few decades (Putnam, 2000). Using bowling as an example, Putnam describes how despite more Americans bowling than ever before, the number of people participating in bowling leagues has steadily declined. One of the ways in which Putnam attempts to explain this gradual disengagement among Americans is by looking at the influence of technology. For all the wondrous effects of modern technology, there may indeed be a darker side as well.

On the surface, it might appear that we are more connected to one another than ever before. Social media has truly "flattened" the world, enabling instant connections spanning continents, mountains, and oceans. We can reconnect with old friends, whom we haven't spoken to in decades. And we can stay in touch with loved ones, even if they're traveling to the most remote areas in the world. On a personal level, I find technology to be exciting and believe that in balance and moderation, it makes the world a better place. But peeling back the layers, we start to see some problems.

A core problem with technology is that it has the potential to pull people apart. Not on the surface of course, but in terms of the deep, genuine connections that play such a critical role in our mental well-being. Recent studies support the notion that despite the ease of connection that exists these days thanks to technology, the quality of those connections has suffered. In America today, surveys show that people report having fewer close and genuine connections than they had even twenty years ago (McPherson, 2006). Worse yet, a quarter of all Americans report feeling that they have no one to confide in, with the problem seemingly getting worse with each passing year.

Given the above findings, it's perhaps not surprising then that rates of depression and anxiety are on the rise, with levels of well-being and happiness stagnating or even declining. The solution to this problem? Increasing the quality of our connections to those around us. By nurturing the social relationships we have, and fostering greater closeness with the important people in our lives, we will harness the immense power of connection to change our lives and increase our happiness. But before we start making those changes, let's first briefly discuss some of the exciting benefits of social connection.

CONNECTION: GOOD FOR OUR MINDS

One of the key distinctions between happy people and those who are less happy is the quality of their interpersonal relationships. Indeed, one of the strongest and most reliable findings in the psychological literature is that happy people are remarkably adept at fostering and nurturing their relationships. On the whole, happy individuals tend to have closer friendships, more satisfying romantic relationships, and more fulfilling family lives. Although it might appear that these benefits are merely byproducts of a person's being happy, the research suggests a more nuanced truth. Indeed, studies suggest that the relationship between happiness and social connection is bidirectional, such that improving our interpersonal relationships offers a reliable and powerful path to becoming a happier person.

Individuals with high social support and connection tend to be significantly happier and more satisfied with their lives (Lyubomirsky, 2007; Lyubomirsky, King, & Diener, 2005). On average, they have significantly lower levels of depression and anxiety than those with less social support. Socially connected individuals are better able to cope with stressful events, and bounce back from setbacks more effectively. Their overall stress level appears to be lower, and their overall quality of life tends to be higher. On the whole, copious amounts of research now support the notion that if we want to become a happier person, it pays to cultivate our interpersonal relationships. But it turns out that beyond helping ourselves emotionally and psychologically, relationships are also good for our health.

CONNECTION: GOOD FOR OUR HEALTH

I completed my pre-doctoral psychology internship at a Veteran's Hospital in Loma Linda, California. Having grown up in New York, and living in the San Francisco Bay Area thereafter, it was initially a bit of a culture shock living in California's so-called "Inland Empire." But I quickly adjusted, and in time I grew quite fond of the area. I remember how one of the first things that struck me was how healthy everyone seemed. Looking around, you'd barely see anyone smoking cigarettes. Red meat was practically nowhere to be found on any menus. And people seemed to walk everywhere by foot, quite different from the rest of us in California.

I soon learned that the residents of Loma Linda, specifically those in the Seventh-Day Adventist community, were a bit of a special breed. Along with just a handful of other communities around the world, they were part of a so-called "Blue Zone," an area in which residents live unusually longer lifespans than most anywhere else (Beuttner, 2010). Other "Blue Zone" communities include Sardinia (Italy), Okinawa (Japan), Icaria (Greece), and the Nicoya Peninsula (Costa Rica). You'll notice that these communities may seem quite different from one another. And indeed, their customs, social structure, and diets are very diverse. But they share a few notable similarities. And right at the top of the list: A strong and pervasive emphasis on social connection and family support.

Inspired by the findings in the "Blue Zones" around the world, scientists have looked deeper into the impact of social connection in our own lives. The findings have been nothing short of remarkable. For example, in a study looking at over 300,000 individuals in the United States, researchers found that close social connection was associated with a 50% decrease in mortality compared to individuals with weaker social bonds (Holt-Lunstad, 2010). This was found to be on par with a number of other risk factors for mortality, including smoking, substance abuse, and exercise habits. In fact, the researchers found that poor social support carried twice the risk of obesity.

In addition to longer life expectancy (House, 1988), strong social support has now been connected to improvements in immune system functioning, along with a lower risk of getting sick (Pressman et al., 2005). It has also been shown to improve sleep quality and quantity, with lonelier people suffering from poorer sleep relative to their socially bonded peers.

Even in the case of chronic and significant health problems, social support plays an important role. One study of heart attack victims recovering in the hospital found that longevity increased with each visitor they received. Conversely, those who did not receive visitors were far more likely to die prematurely (Luskin, 2002). Strong social support may even reduce inflammation in our body, which may account for some of its power across all these different areas.

CONNECTION: GOOD FOR OUR LIVES

Clearly, social connection plays a crucial role in bettering our lives. It even improves our performance at the workplace. Returning for a moment to the men of the Grant Study we discussed earlier, you might be surprised to learn that those with warmer interpersonal connections were found to earn significantly more money than those with less closeness in their lives. In fact, when George Vaillant compared participants who had the strongest connections with those who had the weakest connections, he found that they earned substantially more money during their peak income years. How much more? A whopping $141,000 per year!

Social support and interpersonal connection helps us in a variety of ways. It gives us emotional support when we are struggling, along with practical and tangible support when we are in need. For this reason, people with strong social support have been found to have lower stress levels overall, along with a higher volume of positive emotional experiences. There is even research showing that social connection can resist the strongest barrier to happiness, hedonic adaptation.

You'll recall from Chapter 2 how hedonic adaptation leads us to become increasingly "immune" over time to positive changes in our circumstances (think of the poor, unfortunate lottery winners we discussed earlier). Well it appears that social relationships are an exception, with research showing that positive interpersonal connection is less susceptible to this notion of adaptation. So rather than invest our energy in trying to win the lottery or purchase that beautiful new car, we're better off investing in our relationships with others.

With this in mind, let us now turn our attention to strengthening our connections with those around us. As you'll recall, what matters most is the quality of our connections, rather than the quantity. Whether it's with our spouse, our children, our friends, or our colleagues, we can all reap the benefits of improved connection.

CONNECTION PRACTICES

Connection Practice #1: Gratitude Letter and Visit

The next exercise we'll be practicing is called the "Gratitude Letter and Visit," which is also adapted from the excellent work of Martin Seligman (2005). Although it could just as easily fit in the "Path of Gratitude," the power of this exercise to transform our interpersonal connection underscores its placement in this chapter. **As the name suggests, you'll be writing a letter expressing thanks to someone important in your life, and delivering the letter to that person.** In my own experience of working with patients, this exercise has been described as being incredibly powerful. Some have even described it as "life-changing," and say that it has transformed relationships with others in their lives. In terms of benefits, this exercise has been shown to decrease symptoms of depression, while boosting overall happiness and well-being.

Instructions: We all have people in our lives – friends, parents, teachers, mentors, colleagues, coaches, bosses, and so forth – who have helped us throughout the years. **Think about someone in your life who has helped you along the way, but whom you have never properly thanked.** For the purpose of this exercise, think about an individual who lives near enough to you such that you can visit them in the next few weeks. **Write a detailed and thorough letter of gratitude towards this person, expressing your feelings towards them.** Thank them for all that they have done for you, and how their kindness impacted your life. Revise the letter as needed, and when you feel satisfied with it, set up a meeting with that individual but don't yet tell them the true purpose of your visit. When you meet this person, please either read them the letter aloud or have them read it in your presence. Talk to them about what it was like for them, and share your feelings to them as well. After doing this exercise, write a brief reflection about what the experience was like for you, and how it felt.

As you read the instructions, you may notice yourself feeling excited, or you may notice some nervousness or anxiety creeping up. And that's OK. Most people who I've worked with using this gratitude exercise initially feel some nervousness about completing it, but as mentioned earlier it turns out to have some of the most profound effects on the lives of those who do complete it.

You may also be wondering about the effects of writing a gratitude letter but not sending it, or not delivering it in person. The good news is

(Continued)

that studies have shown that the mere act of writing a letter like this can boost happiness and well-being (Lyubomirsky, 2007). But for the purpose of this exercise, I would definitely encourage you to try and identify someone to whom you can deliver the letter in person because it makes the experience that much more powerful. In the future, you might choose to vary your gratitude letters between these styles, which as we discussed earlier in this chapter can help keep things fresh and maximize helpfulness.

How this exercise works: We've learned about the power of gratitude in this chapter, and we've discussed how the interpersonal component of gratitude may be the most potent ingredient of practicing gratitude. Well, this exercise is essentially interpersonal gratitude on turbo power. Not only are we reflecting on, and identifying people to whom we feel grateful. We are expressing it directly to them in both written and verbal form, thus opening the gateway for increased closeness and connection with that individual.

Getting started: I recommend using a separate piece of paper to write your letter (or better yet, using a computer so that you can edit as needed), but to get started I invite you to reflect on a few people whom you might have interest in writing your letter to. Think about someone who has helped you along the way, but whom you wish to thank in an in-depth and heartfelt way. Use the space below to jot down some ideas, and to start formulating the basis of your gratitude letter:

- Whom do I feel gratitude towards?

  _____

- What does this person mean to me?

  _____

- What did he/she do to help me?

  _____

- What would I like to say to this person?

  _____

- What emotions come up as I reflect on this person?

  _____

- How is my life different because of this person?

  _____

Connection Practice #2: Unplug and Connect

Though technology has transformed our world in numerous positive ways, it nonetheless appears that there is no substitute for genuine face-to-face interpersonal connection. This sort of connection nourishes us, and has been shown to improve both mental and physical health.

Unfortunately, despite its importance, some research suggests that the depth of our social connections has begun to fray. On the one hand, we are more connected than ever; yet at the same time, we seem to have traded quality for quantity. As the "slow food" movement has been an alternative to fast food, perhaps we too are in need of a "slow relationship" movement to restore the quality of our connections. This next exercise invites you to slow down, unplug, and connect in a more meaningful way.

Instructions: Reflect for a moment on the presence of technology in your life. From your smartphone to your tablet, and from your computer to your television, think about the level of interaction you have on a daily basis with technology. Consider how often we are around others, yet nonetheless find ourselves distracted by these influences. We check our emails, respond to messages, and check sports scores. The pull is strong for many of us, and yet it can take us away from the things that matter most in our life.

For the next week, choose one interpersonal activity and commit to making it "media-free." No smartphones, no television shows, and no texting, just you and the other person. This could mean going out to dinner with your spouse, sharing a lunch with a colleague, or going on a hike with a friend. Whatever you choose, commit to spending your time free from technological distractions and focus more fully on the other person. Notice what it's like for you, and briefly write down your reactions once you're done.

Connection Practice #3: The Gratitude Report Card

In Chapter 4, we explored the power of gratitude and its ability to transform our lives. In this exercise, we'll harness that power and use it to improve our relationships with those around us. **Just as it can be easier to focus on what is wrong rather than what is right in our own lives, the same holds true when it comes to our relationships.** Whether in our romantic relationships or our friendships, we are all prone from time to time to focus on our frustrations while taking the good things for granted. This next exercise helps to **counteract this tendency to focus on the negative in your interpersonal relationships,** and is called the "Gratitude Report Card."

Instructions: Over the next week, choose one person in your life with whom you have a close relationship, preferably someone whom you see regularly. This may be a romantic partner, a close friend, or a colleague at work. Each day, write down at least one thing that you appreciate about the person, or something they did for which you are thankful. These appreciations can range in size or scope, but the important thing is that you identify at least one thing each day to write down. At the end of the week, have a face-to-face conversation with this person expressing your thanks to them. Share your list with them, and express how much they mean to you and how appreciative you are to have them in your life.

Connection Practice #4:
Active-Constructive Responding

This next exercise provides a powerful tool to help you develop greater closeness and intimacy in your interpersonal relationships. Drawn from the work of psychologist Shelly Gable (2004), active-constructive responding can be used in your romantic relationships, friendships, and connections at work. In her research, Gable came to realize that there had been a great deal of investigation done on negative interpersonal connections. Yet comparatively very little work had been done looking at the way in which people respond to positive news. As it turned out, this variable (how we respond to positive news from others) strongly predicts the quality of our interpersonal relationships.

According to Gable, there are **four ways** in which we can respond to good news from another person: *active-constructive*, *passive-constructive*, *active-destructive*, and *passive-destructive*. Of these four styles, **only active-constructive responding has been shown to improve the quality and closeness of our interpersonal connections.** In fact, research now shows that individuals who regularly utilize active-constructive responding report higher overall happiness levels, greater life satisfaction, and superior interpersonal relationships (Gable, 2004).

What does this look like in real life? Let's pretend for a moment that your significant other or friend comes to you with the good news that they were offered their dream job. According to this line of research, your four possible responses might look something like this:

Active-Constructive: "That's awesome news! I'm so proud of you. What would you like to do to celebrate?"

Passive-Constructive: "Oh, that's swell" (said with little emotion or enthusiasm).

Active-Destructive: "Well that job's going to require longer hours, right? There goes our weekend, I guess."

Passive-Destructive: "Interesting. Now hurry up to get changed, the movie's starting soon."

Over the course of the next week, **notice the way in which you respond to others when they share good news.** Do you tend to respond in an active-constructive manner, helping them to savor and celebrate their success? Or do you sometimes find yourself drifting towards one of the

(Continued)

other three styles? **In the coming days, make a conscious effort to utilize active-constructive when responding towards others in your life.** Whether it's your spouse, a friend, your parent, or your co-worker, see what happens when you respond more in this manner. Just be yourself, be genuine, and feel your connections start to grow stronger.

Connection Practice #5: Loving-Kindness (Part 2)

A few chapters back, we introduced a particular form of meditation called Loving-Kindness, also known as *Metta*. Whereas many of the mindfulness meditations taught earlier in this book emphasized the cultivation of attention, Loving-Kindness is instead aimed at fostering *connection*. Studies of Loving-Kindness have shown that it has the power to instill deep feelings of love, compassion, and happiness within us. Better still, Loving-Kindness has been shown to improve our connection with others, and can even improve our physical health.

When we engaged in Loving-Kindness earlier, we practiced a version of it in which we focused our attention inwards towards ourselves. **In this practice, we will build on that experience, and begin focusing our attention and kindness outwards towards those around us.** Set aside ten or fifteen minutes per day to begin this practice initially, though over time you may choose to increase this timeframe.

Instructions: Begin by sitting in a comfortable position. Sit upright and relaxed, with your hands resting on your lap. **Take three steady and even breaths,** and when you are ready, close your eyes.

- **Continue to breathe, slowly in and slowly out.** Notice the feeling of the air entering through your nose, and observe how it's slightly warmer on the way out.
- **Become aware of your body as you sit.** Feel your body as it makes contact with the support beneath you. Feel your body resting comfortably, and notice any sensations within your body.
- When you are ready, **form an image of yourself in your mind's eye.** Picture yourself as you currently sit, and feel your heart open up. Remind yourself that like anyone else, you wish to live happily and in peace. Connect fully with that intention, and feel a sense of warmth and compassion pour over you.
- Continue to picture yourself as you sit in this moment. **Gently and in silence, repeat the following phrases to yourself:**
  May I be safe.
  May I be happy.
  May I be healthy.
  May I be peaceful and at ease.

(Continued)

- **Take your time,** all the while maintaining the image of yourself in your mind's eye. Allow the feelings of peace and tranquility to sink in, and savor the meaning of the words.

- When you notice your mind wander or your thoughts drift, **simply notice this,** and return to the present moment.

- **When you are ready, form an image now of someone whom it is easy to feel loving kindness towards.** It could be someone from the past or the present, and could be a friend, family member, or even a pet. A simple, positive relationship can work best to start with. Picture that person, and feel your heart open up to them. Remind yourself that like anyone else, you wish for them to live happily and in peace. Connect fully with that intention, and feel a sense of warmth and compassion pour over you.

- **Continue to picture this loved one** as you sit in this moment. Gently and in silence, repeat the following phrases to yourself:

> May you be safe.
>
> May you be happy.
>
> May you be healthy.
>
> May you be peaceful and at ease.

- Once more, fully allow the words to sink in, and feel your heart open up with love and compassion towards yourself and towards this other person. Take a moment to savor this moment.

- When you are ready, gently open your eyes and return to the room.

Lasting Happiness

*"Happiness is not something ready-made. It comes
from your own actions."*

– His Holiness, the Dalai Lama

Maintaining Happiness

By this point, you've probably already achieved meaningful gains in your pursuit of a happier life. Through the skills you've been practicing in reading this book, it's highly likely that you are already feeling a greater sense of connection, purpose, and peace in your life. Indeed, most people who begin incorporating practices such as gratitude or mindfulness boost their overall well-being and happiness in the short-term. But the real key lies in turning these short-term gains into long-term changes.

Happiness is a skill, no different from any other. And like any skill, it requires an ongoing commitment to developing it for it to grow. Think of it like initiating an exercise regimen, or starting a new diet. It's one thing to eat well for a day, a week, or even a month. And it's easy to go to the gym once or twice, only to then stop. Turning these behaviors into sustainable habits is indeed a taller order, and one that requires patience and determination.

My aim in creating this book was to help you not merely become happier for the short-term, like an emotional version of "yo-yo dieting." Rather, I wanted to provide you with the skills needed to lastingly increase your happiness and well-being for the rest of your life. So while the preceding pages have been aimed to teach you the skills and practices needed to achieve a life of happiness, let's turn now to a series of brief tips to help turn happiness into a lasting way of life. In the days and months to come, use these tips as a guide for helping you maintain your habits of well-being as you embark towards the future.

HAPPINESS TIP 1: CONSIDER WHAT'S BEEN HELPFUL

When considering which sorts of happiness tools to continue practicing in the future, there's no better place to look than the recent past. Reflect for a moment on what has been most helpful during this initial effort towards becoming a happier person. Consider which paths to happiness seemed to resonate most for you, and which particular exercises seemed to give you the greatest boost. If, for example, you found that the cultivation of gratitude resonated with you, then that will likely continue to be an important foundational piece to your happiness work as you move forward. Conversely, if you found that the practice of mindfulness was transformative, then that would be a crucial pursuit to continue. Take a moment and reflect on which specific principles and skills were most helpful for you thus far. Make note of them, and commit to maintaining those practices in the days to come.

HAPPINESS TIP 2: PURSUE WHAT FEELS GOOD

As we've discussed throughout this book, true lasting happiness is comprised of more than simply a collection of positive emotions. But we cannot and should not understate the importance of positive emotions in our lives. Indeed, rather than be viewed as frivolous and fleeting, recent research has shown just how crucial positive emotions are to our health and our mind. Findings by psychologists such as Barbara Fredrickson have shown that positive emotions help to "broaden and build" our minds, opening us up to possibilities and creating a cascade of positive outcomes in our lives and our relationships. So as you move forward, reflect on which of the principles and exercises from this book seemed to result in the greatest amount of positive emotions for you. Consider which practices gave you a sense of joy, pleasure, and gratification. These will serve you moving forward, as they will be practices you can turn to for your necessary dose of positivity.

HAPPINESS TIP 3: TURN HAPPINESS INTO HABIT

Building happiness and well-being largely comes down to habit. And though there are many ideas out there about how to develop habits, unfortunately there are just as many misconceptions. One of the most harmful notions that I've encountered is the widespread yet unsupported notion that it takes 21 days for something to turn into habit. Despite having little to no evidence to support this claim, it nonetheless seems to have seeped into our collective consciousness.

Recent research has debunked this theory, with findings suggesting that it takes longer for habits to develop than perhaps previously thought (Lally, 2008, 2009, 2011). On average, researchers found that it takes 66 days for the average person to develop a habit. However, there was a great deal of individual variation among the participants they studied. For some, it took as little as 18 days, but for others it took over *200*! The bottom line is, it takes time and effort to create habits, and happiness is no different in that respect. But through patience and hard work, the rewards are well worthwhile. There are unfortunately no shortcuts when it comes to building happiness, but through conscious and deliberate effort we can turn happiness into a lasting habit.

HAPPINESS TIP 4: FIX WHAT'S WRONG

One useful way to target your happiness skills is to apply them to areas of need in your life. Consider, for example, what sorts of problems you may be struggling with, or what sorts of deficits may exist in your life right now. For example, you may find yourself rushing through life, unable to appreciate the small steps along the way. In this case, mindfulness may be a particularly helpful practice to cultivate. Conversely, you might find yourself being held back by a grudge, unable to let go of longstanding feelings of resentment. In this instance, the path of forgiveness may prove to be especially useful in unlocking happiness and well-being. Take a moment and reflect on any particular problems, or areas of concern, that you would like to rectify. Consider which happiness practices and skills can help address these areas, and begin incorporating these more in your life for an added boost.

HAPPINESS TIP 5: BUILD WHAT'S STRONG

The flip side of "fixing what's wrong" is to instead focus on "building what's strong." This means that rather than focusing on problems and deficits, you harness the strengths and abilities that you already possess. For each of us, certain paths to happiness may come more naturally, whereas others will be more of a challenge. It's important to incorporate both of these ends of the spectrum, including tapping into the areas of strength already within you. So if you're already a giving person, for example, make sure that you continue to incorporate acts of kindness in your future work towards well-being. Conversely, if mindfulness comes naturally to you, continue to foster and grow this practice as you move forward. By continuing to grow and develop the inherent strengths you already possess, you'll be that much closer to a lasting life of happiness and well-being.

Happiness Tip 6: Change Your Brain

A recurring theme throughout this book has been the notion that our brains are dynamic, rather than static. For many years, it was presumed that our brains stopped changing and developing by early adulthood and would remain in a somewhat fixed state thereafter before succumbing to a gradual decline later in life. However, recent research has discredited this notion, and shed light on the powerful changes that our brains continue to experience over the course of our lives.

The human brain weighs approximately 3 pounds. It contains over a trillion brain cells, and over one hundred billion neurons. These neurons are constantly firing, creating new connections and pathways in our brain. Groundbreaking work by individuals such as Jeffrey Schwartz and Rick Hanson has demonstrated the way our brain changes even on a structural level over time. The notion of "self-directed neuroplasticity" reminds us that our brain is shaped over time by our behaviors, and even by our thoughts. The simple reality is that what we do, and how we think, changes our brain over time.

The exciting implication of this line of research is that we hold the power to slowly "rewire" our brain for happiness and positivity over time. Focusing on stress, pain, and anger leads to increased stimulation of the brain regions associated with these states. Conversely, experiencing happiness, joy, and tranquility activates the brain areas connected to these emotions. Over time, as we continue to foster these habits of well-being, our brain changes accordingly.

Happiness Tip 7: Be a Scientist

The program for well-being described in this book is based on the latest scientific findings on happiness. Each of the principles and exercises contained in the chapters were created according to the latest research on happiness. However, it's important to remember that research tends to be conducted in order to determine what works best for *most* people. You are not most people; you are an individual, with your own unique values, experiences, goals, and preferences.

I therefore encourage you to keep an open mind, and to be receptive to the various suggestions and strategies introduced in this book. However, I also invite you to think critically, and to carefully consider what works best for you as an individual. For example, we can safely say with confidence that mindfulness (or any other path to well-being described in this book) is a helpful strategy in developing happiness. But we cannot pretend to assume that mindfulness is beneficial for *each and every* person trying to become happier. So keep an open mind, but by all means give yourself permission to disagree with anything I've written in the book, and to individualize your happiness plan accordingly.

THE WOLF WE FEED

When I reflect on building a life of happiness and fulfillment, I'm reminded of an ancient Cherokee legend that tells the tale of a grandfather walking with his grandson. The two walk in silence alongside a stream. Water flows gently nearby, and birds chirp from the trees overhead. A gentle breeze passes through, rustling the tall grass and foliage that surrounds them. The grandfather holds his grandson's hand in his own, as they slowly walk side by side.

After some time, the grandson looked up and asked his grandfather how he had become so wise, so respected, and so happy. Pausing to reflect on the question, the old man looked down at his grandson with kindness. After some thought, he responded. "Grandson," he said, "I have two wolves that are fighting in my heart. One wolf is loving, peaceful, kind, and joyful. The other wolf is angry, hateful, and hurtful. They are constantly fighting each other, trying to win the battle of my heart. It is the same battle every person faces in their heart."

Hearing these words, the grandson became filled with fear. He looked up sheepishly, and asked, "Grandpa, which wolf will win the battle?" The wise man smiled knowingly. He answered back, "the one that I feed."

****

Our own pursuit of happiness is in many ways no different from the dilemma faced by the wise Cherokee elder in this story. We each possess within us the necessary ingredients to achieve a life of happiness or a life of misery, depending on our actions and choices. We can feed the wolf of pain, sorrow, and regret. Or we can feed the wolf of love, compassion, and happiness.

This book has provided you with the necessary ingredients to achieve a life of lasting well-being. By fostering skills such as gratitude, mindfulness, kindness, and forgiveness, you can achieve the life you want. With hard work and effort, I truly believe that the sky is the limit. It's been an immense honor to create and write this book, and it is my sincere hope that it will serve you well in your journey. Thank you for taking the opportunity to read this book, and I wish you health and happiness in the days ahead.

Bibliography

Abel, E. L., & Kruger, M. L. (2010). Smile intensity in photographs predicts longevity. *Psychological Science, 21*, 542–544.

Adams, C. & Leary, M. (2007). Promoting Self-Compassionate Attitudes toward eating among restrictive and guilty eaters. *Journal of Social and Clinical Psychology, 26*, 1120–1144.

Algoe, S. (2010). It's the little things: Everyday gratitude as a booster shot for romantic relationships. *Personal Relationships, 17*(2), 217–233.

Bartlett, M. (2006). Gratitude and prosocial behavior: helping when it costs you. *Psychological Science, 17*(4): 319-325.

Blazer, D. (2005). *The Age of Meloncholy: "Major Depression" and its Social Origin*. Routledge Press.

Boehm, J. & Kubzansky, L. (2012). The heart's content: The association between positive psychological well-being and cardiovascular health. *Psychological Bulletin, 138*, 665–691.

Brickman, P. (1978). Lottery winners and accident victims: Is happiness relative? *Journal of Personality and Social Psychology, 36*, 917–927.

Brown, S. (2003). Providing social support may be more beneficial than receiving it: Results from a prospective study of mortality. *Psychological Science, 14*, 320–327.

Buettner, D. (2010). *Thrive: Finding happiness the blue zones way*. Washington, D.C.: National Geographic.

Buss, D. (1989). Sex differences in human mate preferences: Evolutionary hypotheses tested in 37 cultures. *Behavioral and Brain Sciences, 12*, 1–14.

Carson, J. (2004). Mindfulness-based relationship enhancement. *Behavior Therapy, 35*, 471–494.

Carson, J. (2005). Loving-kindness meditation for chronic low back pain: Results from a pilot trial. *Journal of Holistic Nursing, 23*, 287–304.

Chang E.C., & Sanna, L.J. (2001). Optimism, pessimism, and positive and negative affectivity in middle-aged adults: A test of a cognitive-affective model of psychological adjustment. *Psychology and Aging, 16*, 524–31.

Christakis, N., & Fowler, J. (2011). *Connected: The surprising power of our social networks and how they shape our lives—How your friends' friends' friends affect everything you feel, think, and do*. Back Bay Books.

Creswell, J.D. (2008). Mindfulness meditation training effects on CD4+ T lymphocytes in HIV-1 infected adults: A small randomized controlled trial. *Brain, Behavior, and Immunity, 23*, 184–188.

175

Crocker, J., & Canevello, A. (2008). Creating and undermining social support in communal relationships: The role of compassionate and self-image goals. *Journal of Personality and Social Psychology, 95,* 555–575.

Dane, E. (2010). Paying attention to mindfulness and its effects on task performance in the workplace. *Journal of Management, 37*(4), 997–1018.

Dane, E., & Brummel, B.J. (2013). Examining workplace mindfulness and its relations to job performance and turnover intention. *Human Relations,* Sage Journals.

Danner, D., & Snowdon, D. (2001). Positive emotions in early life and longevity: Findings from the nun study. *Journal of Personality and Social Psychology, 80,* 804–813.

Davidson, R. (2003). Alterations in brain and immune function produced by mindfulness meditation. *Psychosomatic Medicine, 65,* 564–570.

Diener E., Wolsic, B., & Fujita, F. (1995). Physical attractiveness and subjective well-being. *Journal of Personality and Social Psychology, 69,* 120–129.

Diener, E. (1999). Subjective well-being: Three decades of progress. *Psychological Bulletin, 125,* 276–302

Diener, E. (2000). Subjective well-being: The science of happiness and a proposal for a national index. *American Psychologist, 55,* 34–43.

Diener, E., & Biswas-Diener, R. (2008). *Happiness: Unlocking the mysteries of psychological wealth.* Oxford: Blackwell Publishing.

Diener, E., Horwitz, J., & Emmons, R. (1985). Happiness of the very wealthy. *Social Indicators Research, 16,* 263–274.

Dillon, K., Minchoff, B., & Baker, K. (1985). Positive emotional states and enhancement of the immune system. *International Journal of Psychiatry in Medicine, 15,* 13–18.

Dunbar, R. (2003). Psychology: Evolution of the Social Brain. *Science, 302,* 1160–1161.

Dunn, E.W. (2008). Spending money on others promotes happiness. *Science, 319*(5870): 1687–1688.

Emmons, R. (2007). *Thanks! How practicing gratitude can make you happier.* New York: Houghton Mifflin Company.

Emmons R.A., & McCullough, M.E. (2003). Counting blessings versus burdens: An experimental investigation of gratitude and subjective well-being in daily life. *Journal of Personality and Social Psychology, 84,* 377–389.

Emmons, R.A., & Shelton, C.M. (2002). Gratitude and the science of positive psychology. In Snyder, C.R., & Lopez, S.J. (eds.). *Handbook of Positive Psychology,* 459–471. Oxford: Oxford University Press.

Eysenck, M. (1990). *Happiness: Fact and myths.* Hove, UK: Lawrence Erlbaum.

Flook et al. (2013). Mindfulness for teachers: A pilot study to assess effects on stress, burnout and teaching efficiency. *Mind, Brain and Education, 7*(3), 182–195.

Frankl, V. (1946). *Man's Search for Meaning.* Vienna, Austria.

Fredrickson, B. (2001). The role of positive emotions in positive psychology: The broaden-and-build theory of positive emotions. *American Psychologist, 56,* 218–226.

Fredrickson, B. (2004). The broaden-and-build theory of positive emotions. *Philosophical Transactions of the Royal Society, 359,* 1367–1377.

Fredrickson, B. (2009). *Positivity: Top-notch research reveals the 3 to 1 ratio that will change your life.* Harmony Press.

Freedman, J. (1978). *Happy people: What happiness is, who has it, and why.* New York: Harcourt Brace Jovanovic.

Fowler, J., & Christakis, N. (2010). Cooperative behavior cascades in human social networks. *Proceedings of the National Academy of Sciences, 107*(12), 5334–5338.

Fox, E. (2013). *Rainy brain, sunny brain: The new science of optimism and pessimism.* UK: Arrow Press.

Gable, E. L., Reis, H. T., Impett, E. A., & Asher, E. R. (2004). Capitalizing on daily positive events. *Journal of Personality and Social Psychology, 87.*

Germer, C. (2009). *The mindful path to self-compassion.* The Guilford Press.

Gilbert, D. (2006). *Stumbling on happiness.* New York: Knopf.

Giltay, E.J., Geleijnse, J.M., Zitman, F.G., Hoekstra, T., & Schouten, E.G. (2004). Dispositional optimism and all-cause and cardiovascular mortality in a prospective cohort of elderly Dutch men and women. *Archives of General Psychiatry, 61,* 1126–1135.

Giltay, E.J., Kamphuis, M.H., Kalmijn, S., Zitman, F.G., & Kromhout, D. (2006). Dispositional optimism and the risk of cardiovascular death: The Zutphen elderly study. *Archives of Internal Medicine, 166,* 431–436.

Giltay, E.J., Zitman, F.G., Kromhout, D. (2006). Dispositional optimism and the risk of depressive symptoms during 15 years of follow-up: the Zutphen Elderly Study. *Journal of Affective Disorders, 91,* 45–52.

Hanson, R. (2009). *Buddha's brain: The practical neuroscience of happiness, love, and wisdom.* Oakland: New Harbinger Publications.

Harker, L., & Keltner, D. (2001). Expressions of positive emotion in women's college yearbook pictures and their relationship to personality and life outcomes across adulthood. *Journal of Personality and Social Psychology, 80,* 112–124.

Hart, S.L., Vella, L., & Mohr, D.C. (2008). Relationships among depressive symptoms, benefit-finding, optimism, and positive affect in multiple sclerosis patients after psychotherapy for depression. *Health Psychology, 27*(2), 230–8.

Hirsch, J.K., Conner, K.R., & Duberstein, P.R. (2007). Optimism and suicide ideation among young adult college students. *Arch Suicide Research, 11*(2), 177–85.

Hirsch, J.K., & Conner, K.R. (2006). Dispositional and explanatory style optimism as potential moderators of the relationship between hopelessness and suicidal ideation. *Suicide and Life-Threatening Behavior, 36,* 661–669.

Holt-Lunstad, J. (2010). Social relationships and mortality risk: A meta-analytic review. *PLoS Medicine, 7.*

Hölzel, B.K., et al. (2011). Mindfulness practice leads to increases in regional brain gray matter density. *Psychiatry Research: Neuroimaging, 191*(1), 36–43.

House, J.S., Landis, K.R., & Umberson, D. (1988). Social relationships and health. *Science, 241,* 540–545.

Ivanowski, B., & Malhi, G.S. (2007). The psychological and neurophysiological concomitants of mindfulness forms of meditation. *Acta Neuropsychiatrica, 19,* 76–91.

Kabat-Zinn, J. (2013). *Full catastrophe living: Using the wisdom of your body and mind to face stress, pain, and illness.* Bantam Books.

Kahneman, D., & Deaton, A. (2010). High income improves evaluation of life but not emotional well-being. *Proceedings of the National Academy of Sciences, 107*(38): 16489–16493.

Kaniel, R., & Robinson, D. (2011). The importance of being an optimist: Evidence from labor markets. *National Bureau of Economic Research Working Paper.*

Karremans, J.C., Van Lange, P.A.M., & Holland, R.W. (2005). Forgiveness and its associations with prosocial thinking, feeling, and doing beyond the relationship with the offender. *Personality and Social Psychology Bulletin, 31,* 1315–1326.

Kashdan, T. (2006). Gratitude and hedonic and eudaimonic well-being in Vietnam war veterans. *Behaviour Research and Therapy, 44*(2), 177–199.

Kelly, A. (2009). Soothing oneself and resisting self-attacks: The treatment of two intrapersonal deficits in depression vulnerability. *Cognitive Therapy Research, 33,* 301–313.

Kelly, A.C., Zuroff, D.C., Foa, C.L., & Gilbert, P. (2010). Who benefits from training in self-compassionate self-regulation? A study of smoking reduction. *Journal of Social & Clinical Psychology,* 29(7), 727–755.

Kessler, R. (1994). Lifetime and 12-month prevalence rates of DSM-III-TR psychiatric disorders in the United States: Results from the national comorbidity survey. *Archives of General Psychiatry, 51,* 8–19.

Keng, S. (2011). Effects of mindfulness on psychological health: A review of empirical studies. *Clinical Psychology Review, 31,* 1041–1056.

Killingsworth, M., & Gilbert, D. (2010). A wandering mind is an unhappy mind. *Science, 330,* 932.

King, L.A. (2001). The health benefits of writing about life goals. *Personality and Social Psychology Bulletin, 27,* 798–807.

King, L., & Miner, K. (2000). Writing about the perceived benefits of traumatic events: Implications for physical health. *Personality and Social Psychology Bulletin, 26,* 220–230.

Koo, M., Algoe, S., Wilson, T., & Gilbert, D. (2008). It's a wonderful life: Mentally subtracting positive events improves people's affective states, contrary to their affective forecasts. *Journal of Personality and Social Psychology, 95,* 1217–1224.

Lally, P. (2011). Experiences of habit formation: A qualitative study. *Psychology, Health & Medicine, 16*(4), 484–489.

Lally, P. (2009). How are habits formed: Modeling habit formation in the real world. *European Journal of Social Psychology, 40*(6), 998–1009.

Lally, P., van Jaarsveld, C.H.M., Potts, H.W.W. & Wardle, J. (2008). How are habits formed: Modelling habit formation in the real world. *European Journal of Social Psychology, 40,* 998–1009.

Lambert, N.M. (2010). Benefits of expressing gratitude: Expressing gratitude to a partner changes one's view of the relationship. *Psychological Science, 21*(4), 574–580.

Lane, R.E. (2000). *The loss of happiness in market democracies.* New Haven: Yale University Press.

Lawler, K.A., Younger, J.W., Piferi, R.L., Jobe, R.L., Edmondson, K.A., & Jones, W.H. (2005). The unique effects of forgiveness on health: An exploration of pathways. *Journal of Behavioral Medicine, 28,* 157–167

Lieberman, M. (2013). *Social: Why our brains are wired to connect.* Crown Publishing

Lucas, R.E., Clark, A.E., Georgellis, Y., & Diener, E. (2003). Reexamining adaptation and the set point model of happiness: Reactions to changes in marital status. *Journal of Personality & Social Psychology, 84*(3), 527–539.

Luks, A. (1988). Doing good: Helper's high. *Psychology Today 22*(10).

Luks, A. (2001). *The Healing Power of Doing Good.* iUniverse.com, Inc.

Luskin, F. (2002). *Forgive for good: A proven prescription for health and happiness.* New York: Harper Collins.

Lyubomirsky, S. (2007). *The how of happiness: A new approach to getting the life you want.* New York: Penguin Books

Lyubomirsky, S., King, L., & Diener, E. (2005). The benefits of frequent positive affect: Does happiness lead to success? *Psychological Bulletin, 131,* 803–855.

Maslow, A. (1962). *Toward a Psychology of Being.* New York: Van Nostrand.

McCullough, M.E. (2001). Forgiveness: Who does it and how do they do it? *Current Directions in Psychological Science, 10*(6), 194–197.

McCullough, M.E., & Witvliet, C.V.O. (2001). The psychology of forgiveness. In S.J. Lopez & C.R. Snyder (ed.), *Handbook of Positive Psychology,* 446–458. New York: Oxford University Press.

McCullough, M.E., Emmons, R.A., & Tsang, J. (2002). The grateful disposition: A conceptual and empirical topography. *Journal of Personality and Social Psychology, 82,* 112–127.

McPherson, M. (2006). Social isolation in America: Changes in core discussion networks over two decades. *American Sociological Review, 71,* 353–375.

Meyer et al. (2007). Happiness and despair on the catwalk: Need satisfaction, well-being and personality adjustment among fashion models. *Journal of Positive Psychology, 2,* 2–17.

Moll, J. et al. (2006). Human fronto-mesolimbic networks guide decisions about charitable donation. *Proceedings of the National Academy of Sciences of the United States of America, 103,* 42.

Moore, A. (2012). Regular, brief mindfulness meditation practice improves electrophysiological markers of attentional control. *Frontiers in Human Neuroscience, 6,* 18.

Murphy, M. J., Mermelstein, L.C., Edwards, K.M., & Gidycz, C.A. (2012). The benefits of dispositional mindfulness in physical health: A longitudinal study of female college students. *Journal of American College Health, 60*(5), 341–348.

Musick, M.A., & Wilson, J. (2003). Volunteering and depression: The role of psychological and social resources in different age group. *Social Science & Medicine, 56.*

Neff, K. (2003). Development and validation of a scale to measure self-compassion. *Self and Identity, 2,* 223–250.

Neff, K. (2009). Self compassion. In Leary, M., & Hoyle, R. (ed.), *Handbook of individual differences in social behavior.* New York: Guilford Press.

Neff, K. (2011). *Self-Compassion: The Proven Power of Being Kind to Yourself.* William Morrow.

Nickerson, C., Schwartz, N., Diener, E., & Kahneman, D. (2003). Zeroing in on the dark side of the American dream: A closer look at the negative consequences of the goal for financial success. *Psychological Science, 14,* 531–536

Norcross, J.C. (2000). Here comes the self-help revolution in mental health. *Psychotherapy, 37,* 370–377.

Oman, D., Thoresen, C.E., & McMahon, K. (1999). Volunteerism and mortality among the community-dwelling elderly. *Journal of Health Psychology, 4*(3).

Ortake, K. (2006). Happy people become happier through kindness: A counting kindnesses intervention. *Journal of Happiness Studies, 7,* 361–375.

Pagano, M. (2009). Helping others and long-term sobriety: Who should I help to stay sober? *Alcoholism Treatment Quarterly, 27,* 38–50.

Pagano, M. (2010). Service to others in sobriety (SOS). *Alcoholism Treatment Quarterly, 28,* 111–127.

Pagano, M., Post, S., & Johnson, S. (2011). Alcoholics anonymous-related helping and the helper therapy principle. *Alcoholism Treatment Quarterly, 29,* 23–34.

Post, S. (2008). *Why good things happen to good people: How to live a longer, healthier, happier life by the simple act of giving.* Broadway Books.

Post, S.G. (2005). Altruism, happiness, and health: It's good to be good. *International Journal of Behavioral Medicine, 12*(2).

Pressman, S. (2005). Loneliness, social network size, and immune response to influenza vaccination in college freshmen. *Health Psychology, 24,* 297–306.

Pressman, S.D., & Cohen, S. (2007). The use of social words in autobiographies and longevity. *Psychosomatic Medicine, 69,* 262–269.

Putnam, R. (2001). *Bowling alone: The collapse and revival of American community.* Touchstone Books, Simon and Schuster.

Ricciardi, E. (2013). How the brain heals emotional wounds: The functional neuroanatomy of forgiveness. *Frontiers in Human Neuroscience, 7,* 839.

Rogers, C. (1961). *On becoming a person.* Boston: Houghton-Mifflin.

Rye, M. (2012). Evaluation of an intervention designed to help divorced parents forgive their ex-spouse. *Journal of Divorce and Remarriage, 53*(3), 231–235.

Sapolsky, R. (1994). *Why zebras don't get ulcers.* Holt Paperbacks.

Scheier, M., & Carver, C. (2010). Optimism. *Clinical Psychology Review, 30,* 879–889.

Schkade, D., & Kahneman, D. (1998). Does living in California make people happy? *Psychological Science, 9,* 340–346.

Schwartz, C.E. et al. (2003). Altruistic Social Interest Behaviors Are Associated with Better Mental Health. *Psychosomatic Medicine, 65.*

Segerstrom, S.C. (2001). Optimism, goal conflict, and stressor-related immune change. *J Behav Med, 24,* 441–467.

Seligman, M.E.P. (2002). *Authentic happiness.* New York: Free Press.

Seligman, M.E.P. (2006). *Learned optimism.* Vintage Press.

Seligman, M.E.P., Rashid, T., & Parks, A.C. (2006). Positive psychotherapy. *American Psychologist, 61,* 774–788.

Seligman, M.E.P., Steen, T.A., Park, N., & Peterson, C. (2005). Positive psychology progress: Empirical validation of interventions psychology progress: Empirical validation of interventions. *American Psychologist, 60,* 410–421.

Shapiro, S., Oman, D., Thoresen, C., Plante, T., & Flinders, T. (2008). Cultivating mindfulness: effects on well-being. *Journal of Clinical Psychology, 64*(7), 840–862.

Stone, A. (1994). Daily events are associated with a secretory immune response to an oral antigen in men. *Health Psychology, 13,* 440–446.

Thompson, B., & Waltz, J. (2008). Self-compassion and PTSD symptom severity. *Journal of Traumatic Stress, 21,* 556–558.

Tindle, H. (2009). Optimism, cynical hostility, and incident coronary heart disease and mortality in the women's health initiative. *Circulation, 120,* 656–662.

Trivers, R. (1971). The evolution of reciprocal altruism. *Quarterly Review of Biology, 46,* 35–57.

Tugade, M., & Fredrickson, B. (2004). Resilient individuals use positive emotions to bounce back from negative emotional experiences. *Journal of Personality and Social Psychology, 86,* 320–333.

Vaillant, G. (2012). Triumphs of experience: The men of the Harvard grant study. Belknap Press.

Weinstein, N. (2009). A multi-method examination of the effects of mindfulness on stress attribution, coping, and emotional well-being. *Journal of Research in Personality, 43,* 374–385.

Wengle, H. (1986). The psychology of cosmetic surgery: A critical overview of the literature. *Annals of Plastic Surgery, 16,* 435–443.

Williams, M., & Penman, D. (2011). *Mindfulness: An eight-week plan for finding peace in a frantic world.* Rodale Press.

Wink, P., & Dillon, M. (2007). Do generative adolescents become healthy older adults? In S. Post (ed.), *Altruism and health.* New York: Oxford.

Witvliet, C.V.O. (2001). Forgiveness and health: Review and reflections on a matter of faith, feelings, and physiology. *Journal of Psychology and Theology, 29,* 212–224.

Witvliet, C.V.O., Ludwig, T.E., & Vander Laan, K.L. (2001). Granting forgiveness or harboring grudges: Implications for emotions, physiology, and health. *Psychological Science, 12,* 117–123.

Wood, A. (2009). Gratitude influences sleep through the mechanism of pre-sleep cognitions. *Journal of Psychosomatic Research, 66*(1), 43–48.

Wood, A. (2008). The role of Gratitude in the development of social support, stress, and depression: Two longitudinal studies. *Journal of Research in Personality, 42*(4), 854–871.

Wood, A. (2010 (in press)). Gratitude and well-being: A review and theoretical integration. *Clinical Psychology Review.*

Worthington, E.L., Jr., Witvliet, C.V.O., Pietrini, P., & Lerner, A.J. (2007). Forgiveness, health, and well-being: A review of evidence for emotional versus decisional forgiveness, dispositional forgivingness, and reduced unforgiveness. *Journal of Behavioral Medicine, 30,* 291–302.

Zahn, R. (2009). The neural basis of human social values: Evidence from functional MRI. *Cerebral Cortex, 19,* 276–283.